SHAKESPEARE'S SONNETS
DATED

SHAKESPEARE'S SONNETS DATED

AND OTHER ESSAYS

LESLIE HOTSON

New York
OXFORD UNIVERSITY PRESS
1949

Printed in Great Britain by Richard Clay and Company, Ltd.,
Bungay, Suffolk

CONTENTS

v

CONTENTS

ILLUSTRATIONS

vii

ILLUSTRATIONS

THE MURDER OF HENRI III

JACKSON'S EGG

PREFATORY NOTE

Most of the work in this collection of essays is new. For the privilege of reprinting papers, some of them here slightly revised, that have appeared elsewhere, I have to thank the editors of *The Times*, the *Atlantic Monthly*, the *Yale Review*, the *Sewanee Review*, and the *Spectator*. Detailed acknowledgements will be found noted in an appendix. The officers and staffs of the Public Record Office, the British Museum, the Library of Congress, and the Folger Shakespeare Library have done much to facilitate my work. To the Rockefeller Foundation I am indebted for the grant of a year's fellowship in the Humanities, which gave me the opportunity of once more picking up the threads of Shakespearean research after the War. As always, my greatest and never-failing source of encouragement has been my wife, to whom these studies are offered.

L. H.

SHAKESPEARE'S SONNETS
DATED

SHAKESPEARE'S SONNETS DATED

EVEN IN this age of ours, Science—good luck to it—has no corner in discovery. History, Biography, Literature: these, too, hold important secrets which may still be brought to light. And for the general reader, the processes of discovery in these fields are more interesting than those of science, both because he can more readily follow them, and because their results are more human.

Here we shall look over the shoulder of the master poet of the modern era, Shakespeare, as he views stirring events as they pass, and transmutes them into literature. We shall discover his response to his world's narrow escape from total destruction; to the crucial naval battle of the century; to the most signal triumph of engineering; to the assassination of the King of France.

Stranger still, in doing so we shall uncover something the world has never suspected: the fact that Shakespeare's poetic powers were full-grown when he was no more than twenty-five years old. It will be an adventure of discovery in History, Biography, and Literature rolled into one.

In not a few of the Sonnets we find a supreme beauty and power of emotion clothed in thought; and since in them we feel drawn closer to the heart of Shakespeare than anywhere in his plays, these poems have aroused enormous interest, almost as much as *Hamlet* has done. But questions about them have also produced volumes of diverse comment, and a perplexing library of conflicting theories. The Sonnets have been called a maze, a labyrinth, the most intricate puzzle in Shakespeare. 'There are many footprints around the cave of this mystery, none of them pointing in the outward direction.' Such is the grim warning of Professor Raleigh.

Just before the War, the danger was pictured for me in a more personal way in Chelsea by Logan Pearsall Smith, whose sane and sensitive judgment is now lost to us. He cautioned me to steer clear of the problem of the Sonnets —a Wandering Wood, he said: an Error's Den. And in his delightful essay *On Reading Shakespeare* he went farther. Here it is not merely 'the Serbonian sonnet-bog, in which armies whole have sunk,' but a region of inky night where not a soul but feels a fever of the mad:

> For listen! the fanatic followers of no less than five ghostly, resurrected Elizabethan Earls are shouting at each other, the two bands of Pembrokians and Southamptonites, each vociferating that their Lord was the inspirer of the Sonnets, while three other bands proclaim the more glorious boast ... that Lord Derby, or Lord Rutland, or Lord Oxford, was the author of them. ... And then, faint and far, as the wind shifts, we hear the ululations of those vaster herds of Baconian believers, as they plunge squeaking down the Gadarene slope of their delusion.

We have been warned! Yet if in the face of all friendly dissuasives we insist on risking our sanity in a fresh attempt, we may draw courage from the remarks of John Benson, on republishing the Sonnets in 1640. Benson was born in Shakespeare's lifetime, before theories about the Sonnets had been invented. And he told his readers, 'You shall find them serene, clear, and elegantly plain; ... no intricate or cloudy stuff to puzzle intellect, but perfect eloquence.' We should also remember that Shakespeare was no mystifier. Both he and his audience knew what he was talking about. George Santayana assures us that the comprehensive poet, such as Shakespeare, 'would be a poet of business. He would have a taste for the world in which he lived, and a clean view of it.'

To begin, then, with the first 'mystery': when were the Sonnets written? No agreement has been reached on this primary question. If we could fix that date, we should have a standpoint from which perhaps to decide what (if anything) there is in the rival theories which see in Shakespeare's friend either the Earl of Southampton or the Earl of Pembroke. We might make a better guess at the identity of the Rival Poet. Above all, what is infinitely more important than anything else, by finding out where the Sonnets belong in the story of Shakespeare's development, we might correct and enlarge our understanding of the greatest poet of the modern world.

Shakespeare has not left us without clues to work upon. Two or three of his sonnets are recognized as carrying external or topical references. Under the influence, however, of diverse preconceptions about their date, critics cannot agree on what events Shakespeare is pointing at. This being so, it is curious that no one has carefully compared these references with the news: that is, with the emergent occurrences of the Europe in which Shakespeare lived as the Soul of the Age—to discover to what notable events between 1585 and 1605, grouped fairly closely together in time, the topical sonnets refer. Possibly historians have not been sufficiently interested in Shakespeare. Or perhaps the literary folk have not troubled to go back to the living contemporary history. Whatever the reason, this obligatory job of collation has not been done.

In comparing the facts of his times with the poet's references, we must begin without a theory, and be ready to follow where the evidence leads. 'If you wish to see the meaning of a thing, look directly into it; for if you think about it, it is altogether missed.' To look directly into the years marching to the close of the Sixteenth Century means for us to look into them so far as we can from Shakespeare's point of view, with Elizabethan anxieties, beliefs, and prejudices. Only in this way shall we see his topical references plain.

I. The Mortall Moone

107

Not mine owne feares, nor the prophetick soule,
Of the wide world, dreaming on things to come,
Can yet the lease of my true loue controule,
Supposde as forfeit to a confin'd doome.
The mortall Moone hath her eclipse indur'de,
And the sad Augurs mock their owne presage,
Incertenties now crowne them-selues assur'de,
And peace proclaimes Oliues of endlesse age.
Now with the drops of this most balmie time,
My loue lookes fresh, and death to me subscribes,
Since spight of him Ile liue in this poore rime,
While he insults ore dull and speachlesse tribes.
    And thou in this shalt finde thy monument,
      When tyrants crests and tombs of brasse are spent.

This is the chief 'dating sonnet,' and it has been called the most difficult of all. And here I think we shall find that the world has been led down a false trail by assuming that *the mortall Moone* means Queen Elizabeth, and that *hath her eclipse indur'de* means either that she is dead, or that she has survived a dangerous crisis in her life.

To read it as 'the Queen is dead' would place this sonnet in 1603. Beyond the unnatural callousness of writing '*the* Moone' instead of ' *our* Moone,' there are other serious objections to this interpretation. For the Elizabethan vogue of sonnet-writing, 1603 is too late. It is also too late in Shakespeare's career to suit with the style and tone of his sonnets, in one of which he describes himself as a beginner, wielding a 'pupil pen.' Most critics have therefore taken the second meaning—that *the mortall Moone* is the living Queen.

But this theory will not stand the test of the times. All the English poets write of their beloved Queen in terms approaching adoration. She is a goddess come to earth, a heaven-born Astræa. 'This is that Queen, as writers truly say, That God had marked down to live for aye.' She is Diana. 'Time weares her not . . . Mortalitie belowe her orbe is plaste.' Her word is *Ever the Same*. Her loyal subjects neither wish nor dare to remind her that she is mortal. 'Wee are afraid,' says John Donne, 'to speake to the great men of this world of their death, but nourish in them a vaine imagination of immortality.' Loathing the advances of creeping Time, Elizabeth carries her aversion to the mention of death to strange lengths. Informed by the unwary Lord North that a certain covered pie is called a 'coffin,' she bursts out in anger, 'And are you such a fool, to give a pie such a name?'

Mortal, moreover, bears a meaning even more hideous, and one equally common in Shakespeare's works: *deadly*, *death-dealing*. 'Mortal poison,' 'mortal murders,' 'mortal butcher,' 'mortal rage.' To fancy Shakespeare deliberately writing of his 'imperiall Votresse' not only that she is *mortal*, but that she has been obscured by an eclipse, is to imagine him a greater fool than Lord North.

If it cannot be Elizabeth, what then is this *mortall Moone*? For more than three centuries the answer has vainly stared us in the face. It is the *deadly Spanish Armada of 1588*—the mightiest floating army that the world had ever seen—which in its menacing moon-shaped line of battle appeared in the English Channel, only to be shattered by the drum-fire of Elizabeth's heavy guns, and driven northward away before an irresistible gale into ignominy, disaster, and eclipse.

> *The Spanish Fleet did flote in narrow Seas*
> *And bend her ships against the English shore.*
> Theodore Beza, *Ad Serenissimam Elizabetham Angliae Reginam*, 1588.

. . . their fleete was placed in battell araie, after the maner of a Moone cressant, being readie with her horns & hir inward circumference to receiue either all, or so manie of the English nauie, as should giue her the assault.
> Petruccio Ubaldino, *A Discourse concerninge the Spanish fleete*, 1588.

Don Pedro. Cast our Fleet
Into a wide, and Semi-circled Moone:
And if we can but once incompasse them,
Wee'll make the Sea their Graues.
> Thomas Heywood, *If you know not me*, Part 2, (1606) (published 1632).

That fleet, which with the Moone for vastnesse stood,
Which all the earth, which all the sea admires,
Amaz'd to see on waves a Moone of wood.
> Phineas Fletcher, *The Locusts*, 1627.

6

... like your invincible Armado's, which in their first appearance make a mighty Moone, but are burnt and confounded in the end.

> Richard Carpenter, *Experience, Historie, and Divinitie,* 1642.

... a horned Moone of huge and mighty shippes. ... But all is vaine: for the breath of the Lords mouth hath dimmed the brightnesse of her Moone, and scattered those proud shippes.

> J[ames] L[ea], *The Birth, Purpose and mortall Wound of the Romish holie League,* 1589.

The mortall Moone hath her eclipse indur'de. That Shakespeare, like James Lea in his triumphant political cartoon, is here in Sonnet 107 celebrating the eclipse suffered by the deadly 'Moone of huge and mighty shippes' now appears, as John Benson might say, serene, clear, and elegantly plain.

But if in any mind there lingers a doubt, it is set at rest by Shakespeare himself. For in his dealing with another great sea-fight which likewise marked a turning-point in history, we now discover him repeating his metaphor of an eclipsed moon for a defeated fleet. This was the Battle of Actium on the Ionian Sea, in which the huge heavy galleys of Antony and Cleopatra, crowded with people and not well manned, were beaten by the smaller, nimbler, battle-wise craft of Octavius and Agrippa. Like every Englishman reading his Plutarch, Shakespeare would mark that historic parallel with the Armada fight.

The ranked fleets of beaked galleys faced each other in curving line-abreast. After Agrippa had lured out Antony's left wing from its well-nigh impregnable position and the fierce struggle had been joined, Cleopatra

'MAPPE' SHOWING ARMADA 'MOON'

From *The Birth, Purpose and mortall Wound of the Romish holie League*
by J[ames] L[ea], 1589

and her Egyptian contingent of sixty huge ships, shame-
fully followed by her enslaved Antony, 'fled From that
great face of Warre, whose seuerall ranges Frighted each
other.' The brave remnant fought on to defeat.

> *Enobarbus.* Alacke, alacke.
> *Canidius.* Our Fortune on the Sea is out of breath,
> And sinkes most lamentably.

This anguished avowal is later echoed by the 'noble ruin',
Antony. Plunged in black remorse over their ominous
defeat, he cannot hear Cleopatra:

> *Cleo.* Haue you done yet?
> *Ant.* Alacke our Terrene Moone is now Eclipst,
> And it portends alone the fall of *Anthony.*

Terrene is a short form of *Mediterranean,* favourite with
the geographer Ortelius and the dramatist Marlowe: 'not
far from Alexandria, Whereas the Terrene and the Red
Sea meet.' The mighty battle-crescent of their Mediterranean fleet has suffered eclipse, giving infallible omen of
Antony's fall.

The *mortall Moone* sonnet, then, is Shakespeare on the
Armada. If this capital fact is now evident, we should also
find in the poem some reference to the fatal and wonderful
year, 1588: the menacing, long-prophesied Eighty-Eight,
ever memorable in the world's mind for the destruction
of the Invincible Fleet. For in retrospect the two were
inseparable:

> *The miraculous victory atchieved by the English Fleete*
> *. . . upon the Spanish huge Armada sent in the yeere 1588.*
> Having in part declared the strange and wonderfull
> events of the yeere eightie eight, which hath bene so
> long time foretold by ancient prophesies; we will now

ARMADA 'MOON'

One of the designs for tapestry by Henry Cornelius de Vroom (Haarlem, 1566–1619)

make relation of the most notable and great enterprise
of all others which were in the foresaid yeere atchieved.
> Emanuel van Meteren, *History of the Low
> Countries*, ch. XV (1602).

And whereas the aduersaries made no small accompt
of that Astrologicall prediction, & perhaps trusted in
it . . . we may now safely declare the accomplishment,
by adding a Pentameter, and say
> *Octogesimus octauus mirabilis annus,*
> *Clade Papistarum, faustus vbique pijs.*
[Fifteen Eighty-Eight, that fatal and wonderful year,
Papists' defeat; to the godly, joy everywhere.]
> Dr. William Fulke's dedication to Queen Eliza-
> beth of his *Text of the New Testament*, 1589.

But Thou, Lord . . . madest the year of greatest
expectation, even '88, marvellous by the overthrow of
thine . . . enemies.
> Anthony Rudde, Bishop of St. David's, prayer in
> sermon at Court, April 9, 1596.

The Prediction of Regiomontanus; *Octogesimus
octauus mirabilis Annus*; Was thought likewise accomplished, in the sending of that great Fleet, being the
greatest in Strength, though not in Number, of all that
euer swamme vpon the Sea.
> Francis Bacon, ' Of Prophecies,' *Essayes*, 1625.

Octogesimus Octauus Annus, That same terrible 88.
which came sayling hither in the Spanish Armado.
> Thomas Dekker, *The Wonderfull Yeare*, 1603.

. . . with the Spanish vndoubted hope of Englands
conquest, in the dreadfull yeare of 1588.
> Anthony Mundy, *A Briefe Chronicle*, 1611.

A.D. 1588. We are now come to that fatall yeare, which the *Astrologers* called the *Marveilous yeare*; some said it was the *Climactericall* yeere of the world. And they that trust not in the *liuing God* . . . tooke the opportunitie of this *fatall* yeare as they supposed, now vtterly to overthrow the *Church* of *England* and *State*. Which before they could not doe. The *Pope* and *Spanyard* layd vp all their hopes vpon this yeares *destiny*.

George Carleton, Bishop of Chichester, *A Thank-full Remembrance*, 1624.

Witness that admirable year eighty-eight. . . . It was a year of strange *expectation*, before it came, and of *admiration*, when it was come. Some designed it to be the end of the world, but were deceived. Others designed it to be the doomsday of England, the ruin of our Church and religion, and the funerals of our prince, people, and kingdom, all on one day: but these also through the great mercy of God were deceived.

Thomas Taylor, 'Eighty Eight,' a sermon, 1631.

The year of universal apprehension, in which the world expected the day of doom, or at the least miracles full of peril—such was the year 1588. It had loomed for more than a century, ever since that 'most notorious prophesie' of 1475, attributed either to Johann Stoffler or to Johann Müller of Königsberg (Regiomontanus), and taken up and repeated by Melanchthon:

Tausent fünffhundert achzig acht,
  Das ist das Jar das ich betracht:
Geht in dem die Welt nicht vnder,
  So gschiet doch sonst grosz mercklich Wunder.

These 'Germanical Rhythmes' were expanded into Latin verses, of which the following was one English version:

When from the Virgin Birth a thousand yeares
With full five hundred be compleat and told,
The Eightie Eighth a famous yeare appeares,
Which brings distresse more fatall then of old.
If not in this yeare all the wicked world
Do fall, and land with sea to nothing come;
Yet Empires must be topsie turvie hurl'd,
And extream grief shall be the common summe.

As the time foretold inexorably drew near, this was regarded as 'the onely prophesie of the world.' The embattled Protestants worked out 1588 as the world's 'grand climacterical'—the end of ten cycles of sevens—as follows:

the Captiuitie of Babylon endured 70. yeares, which may be thought too prefigure the Captiuitie of the Gospel in these latter dayes: for from the yeare of our Lord 1518. in the which Martine Luther began truely to preach Gods word, which forthwith became captiue with fire, sworde, and all crueltie, too 1588. are iust .70. yeares, in the whiche yeare .1588. according as *Iohannes Regiomontanus*, . . . *Schonerus, Leouitius*, and other greate learned men agree, some greater thing shall bee done.[1]

Ominous corroboration came from the astronomers. They pointed to 1588's threatening conjunction of the planets Saturn, Jupiter, and Mars; and 'in the selfsame yeere 88 . . the Sunne shall be eclipsed the 16. day of *February* at the change; and shortly after, at the very next full, namely the second day of *March* there shall follow a Totall Eclipse of the Moone.' On top of this, there would be a second 'vniuersall *Eclipse* of the Moon this 88. to befall the 26. day of August.' Three eclipses in one year!

[1] James Sandford, *Houres of Recreation*, 1576.

And the renowned Hermes Trismegistus had laid it down that 'there insue manifold mischiefes in the world when the Sun, and Moone are both eclipsed in one moneth.'

Alarm was so deep and general that books had to be written to combat the auguries of dread. John Harvey devised a discourse 'especially in abatement of the terrible threatenings, and menaces, peremptorily denounced against the kingdoms, and states of the world, this present famous yeere, 1588. supposed the *Greatwoonderfull,* and *Fatall* yeere of our Age.' Ministers were preaching repentance before Judgment, as a 'Preparation against the prognosticated dangers of this yeare 1588.' Broadside ballads and books were printed 'Of the end of the world.' For everything clearly pointed to a present fulfilment of the Gospel prophecy of the Last Day:

> *And there shalbe signes in the sunne and in the moone,*
> *& in the starres: and vpon the earth trouble among the*
> *nations, with perplexitie. The sea and the water shall rore.*
> *And mens heartes shal fayle them for feare, and for*
> *loking after these thinges which shall come on the world.*

Luke 21: 25, 26.

Leonard Wright sums it up:

> who hath not read or hard what wonderful strange eclips of sun & moon, terrible blazing stars, glistering comets, dreadful coniunctions of planets, strange flashing of fire in the elements, & alteration of the heauens, resembling as it were the countenance of the angry Iudge?[1]

Such were the universal fears and auguries of 1588. And the arrogant Spaniards, 'Who by report through all the

---

[1] *A Summons for Sleepers,* 1589.

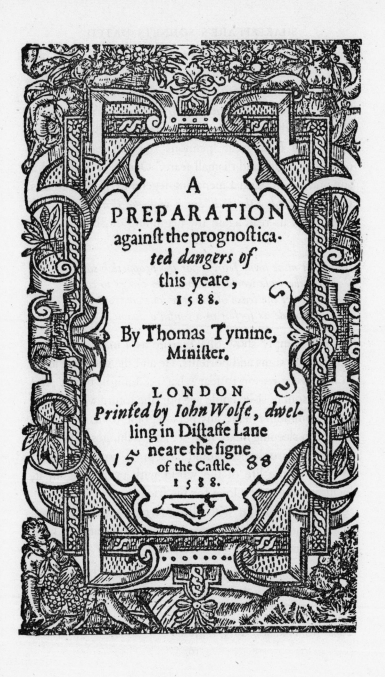

A
PREPARATION
against the prognostica-
ted *dangers of*
this yeare,
1588.

By Thomas Tymme,
Minister.

LONDON
Printed by Iohn Wolfe, dwelling in Distaffe Lane
15 neare the signe 88
of the Castle.
1588.

world, had won The name of conquest ere the fight begun,' assumed that the prophecy would be fulfilled by the
fall of England under the blows of their military might.
To advertise their purpose, and to strike terror into *los
lutheranos*, they painted their England-bound battleships
black, and flew great 'pennons tragicall' bearing 'sad
ostents of death and dismall feare.' One such displayed a
sun and moon, with a menacing legend in Spanish to this
effect: *Yesterday the Full, but Today the Wane.*

Now let us read again the beginning of Shakespeare's
sonnet:

> *Not mine owne feares, nor the prophetick soule,*
> *Of the wide world, dreaming on things to come,*
> *Can yet the lease of my true loue controule,*
> *Supposde as forfeit to a confin'd doome.*

His plays amply show Shakespeare as a man of his age,
believing in signs and portents. He and the world he lived
in had every reason to fear what 1588 might bring. And
that the soul in sleep could see into the future was another
belief commonly held: 'any person going to his rest...his
Soule (in sleeping) may fore-see many thinges to come.'[1]
The doom prophesied would have put a 'confine,' a limit
or end, to the life of the world with everything in it,
including the poet's love for his friend.

But Eighty-Eight with all its terrors and eclipses has
come—and gone! The apprehensions of doomsday have
proved baseless:

> *The mortall Moone hath her eclipse indur'de,*
> *And the sad Augurs mock their owne presage . . .*

---

[1] Pedro Mexia and others, *Treasurie of auncient and moderne
Times* (tr. T. Milles), 1613, I. 476*b*.

The Invincible Armada has suffered defeat: an event, writes
Professor Trevelyan, 'which all Europe at once recognized as a turning point in history.' Instead of cataclysm,
1588 brought to England, and to all Protestant Europe
with her, the rejoicing dawn of certain deliverance. The
relief was indescribable. And in his treatise against
astrology (1601) John Chamber has the prophets of a
black 1588 mocking their own presage:

> It were well that all of that trade had those two
> figures .88. seared in their foreheads, that when they
> meet, they might laugh one at another, as did the
> *Aruspices* in olde time. Howsoeuer they might laugh, it
> was no laughing matter to the Catholike king, and his
> inuincible Nauie, who will be famous for that exploit
> till 88 come againe.

> *Incertenties now crowne them-selues assur'de,*
> *And peace proclaimes Oliues of endlesse age.*

Here is where the modern historian leads us astray. He
likes to call the Armada fight the beginning of Elizabeth's
formal hostilities with Philip, leaving us to think that
Shakespeare's countrymen now knew they were at war.
How totally different was the view of the man on the spot!
For him, the victory of '88 brought not war, but the certain assurance of *peace* for England. There would be no
invasion and butchery, such as the Low Countries suffered
under Alva. No savage civil wars of religion, like those
torturing France. Throughout her reign, whatever forces
she might dispatch to fight her enemies abroad, Elizabeth
was incessantly extolled for keeping her land at peace.

Tom Nashe and Robert Greene give us the characteristic post-Armada sentiment. Nashe writes, 'the Prayers
of the Church of England flie vppe into heauen for her

Maiestie, and returne againe with Oliue-branches in their mouthes . . . to bring tydings of peace and long life vnto her highnesse.' And he calls his Queen 'heauenborne *Elizabeth*, . . . a subiect of wonder, & Peace.'[1] In his triumphant and thankful *Spanish Masquerado* (entered 1 February 1589) Greene borrows from the Bible to exclaim,

> Let Englishmen then, shrouded vnder the wings of the most highest, not feare what thousands can doe against them: nay let them giue thanks to God who hath blest vs with such a Prince as makes vs eate fruites of our own vineyard, and drinke water of our owne welles: our Cities are full of ioy, and our children are seene sporting in the streetes: peace and plentie flourisheth in *England* . . . our mercifull God maketh *ENGLAND* like *EDEN*, a second Paradice.

Elizabeth's great astrologer, Dr. John Dee, addresses her from Bohemia to thank God for 'this wunderfull triumphant Victorie, against your mortall enemies,' and to thank her Majesty for 'calling me . . . hoame, into your British Earthly Paradise, and Monarchie incomparable.'[2] And Francis Bacon, looking back over Elizabeth's reign, saw the Armada 'first beaten in a battle, and then dispersed and wasted in a miserable flight with many shipwrecks; while on the ground and territories of England, peace remained undisturbed and unshaken.'[3]

---

[1] *The Returne of the renowned Caualiero Pasquil of England*, 1589; *The Anatomie of Absurditie*, entered 19 September, 1588.

[2] B.M. MS. Harley 6986, f. 28 (45).

[3] *In Felicem Memoriam Elizabethae* (tr. James Spedding), *Works* (1858) vi. 295, 309.

Now with the drops of this most balmie time,
My loue lookes fresh, and death to me subscribes,
Since spight of him Ile liue in this poore rime,
While he insults ore dull and speachlesse tribes.
And thou in this shalt finde thy monument,
When tyrants crests and tombs of brasse are spent.

The drops of this most balmie time—after the eclipse of the deadly Spanish 'Moone'—have brought life revived and fresh out of the shadow of doom. Balm is the biblical Balm of Gilead or Balsam of Mecca, the prime life-restoring elixir. Its source is the Eastern balsam tree, 'out of which issueth a Gumme of excellent swiftnesse.' As Othello says, 'Drops teares as fast as the Arabian Trees Their Medicinable gumme.' Books were written on the magical healing powers of the drops of balm. Shakespeare often mentions it: 'balme, Earth's soueraigne salue,' 'drop sweet Balme in *PRIAMS* painted wound,' 'balme to heale their wounds,' 'Balme of hurt Mindes.' It is frequent in his fellow-authors: 'the drops of balsamum, that salveth the most dangerous sores' (Dr. Thomas Lodge). 'The tree of life . . .

From that first tree forth flowd, as from a well,
A trickling streame of Balme, most soueraine . . .
Life and long health that gratious ointment gaue,
And deadly woundes could heale, and reare againe
The senselesse corse appointed for the graue.'
                                                    (Spenser)

'*Elizabeth*, who with her English balme, Then much the poysnous biting of that *Spanish* aspe did calme' (Warner). 'The time! O blessed time! Balme to our sorrow!' (Dekker).

Now that the Elizabethans have given us the indispensable background, we are better equipped to attempt a running comment on the thought of Sonnet 107, as follows:

The poet's fear, shared with the whole Protestant world, of the dread cataclysm foretold for 1588, has not been able to put an end to his love. The foe's 'invincible' battle-crescent has, however, met disaster; and the prophets of doom are laughing at their recent fears. Danger of invasion and civil war has vanished as if blown away with the storm that wrecked the beaten Armada. Elizabeth's Englishmen find themselves joy-fully gazing down far vistas of assured peace.

To minds hurt by cruel apprehension and suspense, the miraculous passing of 1588 not only in safety but crowned with victory has come as a life-restoring balm. In this blessed time of deliverance love has renewed its youth. Death, shorn of his terrors, now submits to the poet, whose verse is his passport to immortality. The poet's friend, the subject of his lines, will be remembered when the blazoned crests and tombs of the defeated tyrants Philip and Sixtus are long gone into oblivion.

It is deeply satisfying to find that long before he sang the glory of Agincourt, Shakespeare had begun by record-ing with his 'pupil pen' the overthrow of the Invincible Armada, the eclipse of the Spanish dream of world dominion. To the insatiable monarch—whose inflated motto *The Whole World is Not Enough* Drake found so amusing—Shakespeare gave England's answer, quiet and conclusive:

The mortall Moone hath her eclipse indur'de.

The naval historian may now see Shakespeare's line great with meaning: an utterance proclaiming the death of the old order and the birth of the new. For he tells us that the Armada fight spelled the eclipse of the ancient naval tactics. The Spaniards' fleet was still ranged line-abreast in the *falange*, 'a battle like a halfe Moone,' like the war-ships at Actium. Their classic aim was to fight ship against ship, grapple, board, and settle the issue hand to hand. But the nimbler English never gave them the chance. Howard and Drake, coming down a-weather on them in line-ahead, 'crossing their T,' concentrating crushing broadsides of heavy metal on a selected target, brought not only the eclipse of the 'Moone,' but also the dawn of the modern era at sea.

As soon as we locate the spiritual landscape—the passing of 1588—in which it was written, Shakespeare's 'most difficult' sonnet becomes clear and plain. We see what events he has turned into ideas; and, for the first time, we understand. May not other sonnets that still seem puzzling or obscure behave in the same way?

II. The Riddle of the New-Old Pyramids

123

No! Time, thou shalt not bost that I doe change,
Thy pyramyds buylt vp with newer might
To me are nothing nouell, nothing strange,
They are but dressings of a former sight:
Our dates are breefe, and therefor we admire,
What thou dost foyst vpon vs that is ould,
And rather make them borne to our desire,
Then thinke that we before haue heard them tould:
Thy registers and thee I both defie,
Not wondring at the present, nor the past,
For thy records, and what we see doth lye,
Made more or les by thy continuall hast:
    This I doe vow and this shall euer be,
    I will be true dispight thy syeth and thee.

In this sonnet addressed to Time, Shakespeare nonchalantly declares, 'Thy pyramids built up with newer might to me are nothing novel.' By these ostensibly novel pyramids of old Time he obviously cannot mean structures as stupendous as the Great Pyramid of Gizeh. No monsters like that were set up in his age. But what then *does* he mean? His 'pyramids' is certainly a poser.

Now when a concrete term in Shakespeare offers a puzzle, the most promising method of attacking it has two steps. First, to find out what the word meant to his contemporaries. Second, to acquire some notion of its specific application here by studying any contemporaneous events involving the thing referred to.

If we ask what other Elizabethans meant by 'pyramids,' we are told at once. They habitually broadened its sense to include *slim spires*, and particularly *obelisks*. Out of many examples of this, here are a few: Marlowe describes ships' masts as 'pyramides'; and in Rome his Mephistophilis promises to show Doctor Faustus the great Egyptian obelisk in front of St. Peter's, which he calls the 'high pyramides that Julius Caesar brought from Africa.' Italians, too, often used the term in this looser sense, for in his work on the Vatican obelisk (1586) Pietro Angelio writes in Latin[1] a poetic *Complaint of the Obelisk, that by some it is called a Pyramid*. He has the Obelisk pointing out the obvious differences between the Pyramid and itself, and wondering why people *will* persist in miscalling it a pyramid. Any Englishman brushing up his French in 1593 with John Eliot's lively conversation-book would also come upon the famous Vatican monolith: 'Didst thou

---

[1] *Commentarius de Obelisco*, Romæ 1586.

POPE SIXTUS V
Venetian School, Vatican Gallery

never see the Pyramides which is in Saint Peters Church-yard at Rome?' In *Histriomastix*, a play of 1589, Lord Landulpho says, 'In honour of our Italy we sport ... Our Amphitheatres and Pyramides.' The traveller William Lithgow, in Rome in 1609, says he saw the 'Piramides, some whereof during her former glory were transported from Ægypt.' In short, were you to show Shakespeare Cleopatra's Needle and the Washington Monument today, he would naturally call them both 'pyramids.'

If we now substitute the word *obelisk* in Shakespeare's line—*Thy obelisks built up with newer might*—and at the same time recall Elizabethan news about building, at once a flood of light breaks in. For the mightiest builder in all the world in Shakespeare's time was the enterprising, tenacious, and severe Pope Sixtus V, who reigned from 1585 to 1590. So many were his notable constructions that under his hand Rome rose from its ruins and 'forth-with doubled itself.' His most spectacular and world-famous achievement, however, was the re-erection, as 'monuments of religious magnificence,' of four age-old obelisks. These had been brought from Egypt to Imperial Rome by the Caesars and—all but one—were long since thrown down, broken, and even lost many feet under-ground.

Mighty Sixtus, who regarded himself as one of the two most powerful temporal kings in the world, set up a great Egyptian obelisk in each of the years 1586, 1587, 1588, and 1589. They stand today where he stationed them. The hugest one in existence, which in 1588 he erected by S. Giovanni in Laterano, had been discovered the year before buried in the Circus Maximus, broken into three pieces. This giant of red granite had therefore to be 'born'

23

—extracted from Mother Earth—and then literally 'built,' requiring in its broken state more 'building' than the placing of an entire monolith on a pedestal.

But first in priority, as well as alone in its glory of having survived the centuries unbroken and erect, was the Vatican obelisk, familiarly known as St. Peter's Needle— *la guglia di San Pietro*, 'the largest entire obelisk out of Egypt, and the second in size in the world.' Weighing some 320 tons, it stood near the Basilica, deep in the mud and rubbish of what had once been the *spina* of the race-track of Nero's Circus. The work of taking it down, moving it to its present commanding site, and re-erecting it on a splendid pedestal in 1586, was the first and most dramatic feat to bring universal fame to the Pope's brilliant engineer, Domenico Fontana.

Flocks of important persons hastened to Rome from the corners of Europe to witness the marvellous operation. As the biographer of Sixtus tells us,

> Contemporary letters, reports of the diplomats, the stage-plays—that precious source of history when it is a matter not of establishing facts but of appreciating the trend of opinion,—numberless verses celebrating the event, and even views of the city of Rome published for visitors, by the exaggerated size they give to the obelisk, all witness to the sympathetic interest Europe took in the successful accomplishment of an enterprise which the leading authorities of art and engineering (Michael Angelo and Antonio de Sangallo) had pronounced impossible. Strangers just off the ship ran to see the Needle.[1]

Among the numberless Latin verses flattering the Pope on this superhuman achievement, the ones most amusing

---

[1] Baron J. A. de Hübner, *Sixte-Quint*, vol. ii, 'The Needle.'

'MOVING THE OBELISK'
Fresco Painting, Gallery of Pius IV,
Vatican Library

to Englishmen watching Philip building his Armada were doubtless those by a certain Bucovius, a Pole—in English as follows:

> Since an immovable mass, O excellent Father, obeys thy will, and is now shifted by thy commands . . . since moreover it is wicked for it not to follow thy orders; when even stones go under thy yoke, *may I doubt that the unruly Britons are about to bow their necks?*

If the rhetorical Pole wanted the authentic answer, he would get it from those same unruly British necks in a wicked chorus of 'You may, Bucovius, you may!'

The re-discovery in the following year of the tallest obelisk ever quarried, together with its excavation and its building in 1588 as the *Obelisco Lateranense*, was a fresh 'sensation.' And in 1589 Pope Sixtus was once more in the news with a fourth obelisk, likewise dug up out of the Circus Maximus, which he erected in the Piazza della Madonna del Popolo. This was his last: he died in August 1590.

The topical force of Shakespeare's 'pyramids' for the period about 1589 is now evident. On re-reading the sonnet with our eyes opened to the background of the world news, we can now offer a comprehensible summary, somewhat as follows:

Standing firm himself, the poet scorns the tricks of Time. He declines to join the childish world in its admiration over a nine days' wonder which it regards as a 'strange novelty.' Everybody's talking about the pyramids brought forth—as if produced for their special delight—from the womb of earth by the autocrat of Rome and his engineer. The poet is not impressed. After all, these obelisks, while newly set up, con-

secrated, and dressed with his armorial bearings and Christian crosses by Sixtus, are in fact no new invention, but some 3000 years old, and we had heard about them from historians. Though now palmed off as a novelty on an ignorant world gaping for curiosities, their austere shafts, bearing Time's registers in royal hieroglyphs, were common sights ages ago.

But the poet puts no trust either in Time or in his deceptive memorials. Time's restless pace often destroys his own records, thus making them less. Just now, on the other hand, he has had some lost and forgotten ones dug up, thus making them more. Fickle and unreliable as he thus shows himself, who will believe him? The poet will remain unchanged and a true friend in spite of all that Time the deceiver and destroyer can do.

Notorious events as reported to the Elizabethan world have shown us approximately how Shakespeare's contemporaries would understand the allusions in this sonnet. So far from being metaphorical, intricate, and cloudy (as they seemed to our modern ignorance), they were clear, concrete, and topical. We can easily see now what was conveyed by *pyramids, newer might, novel, dressings of a former sight, admire what thou dost foist upon us that is old*, and *thy registers*.

As for the date of this sonnet, I place it in 1589. Since *pyramids* is in the plural, it cannot have been written before 1587, when the *second* obelisk (S. Maria Maggiore) was set up. The topicality of the term *novel*, meaning new, the latest thing; the phrase *not wondering at the present*; the admired 'birth' of the excavated pyramids of 1588 and 1589 to the satisfaction of a sensation-hungry age in which (as Tom Nashe writes in 1589) 'men hast vnto nouelties, and runne to see new things'; and the present

TITLE-PAGE OF 'DEL MODO TENUTO NEL TRASPOR-
TARE L'OBELISCO VATICANO' BY DOMENICO
FONTANA, 1589

tense of *what thou dost foist upon us*—all these indicate
that the sonnet was written while the obelisks were still
being set up: while, in short, they were 'news.' After the
death of Sixtus in August 1590, the *newer might* of that
powerful figure was a thing of the past, and the Roman
pyramids were no longer either novel or news.

III. THE BLOW OF THRALLED DISCONTENT

Having found that the topicalities of Sonnet 107—*the
mortall Moone*, and of Sonnet 123—the *pyramyds*, lead us
to refer them both pretty closely to the year 1589, let us
now turn to scrutinize the political allusions in the sonnet
which immediately follows the *pyramyds*:

124

Yf my deare loue were but the childe of state,
It might for fortunes basterd be vnfathered,
As subiect to times loue, or to times hate,
Weeds among weeds, or flowers with flowers gatherd.
No it was buylded far from accident,
It suffers not in smilinge pomp, nor falls
Vnder the blow of thralled discontent,
Whereto th'inuiting time our fashion calls:
It feares not policy that *Heriticke*,
Which workes on leases of short numbred howers,
But all alone stands hugely pollitick,
That it nor growes with heat, nor drownes with
    showres.
  To this I witnes call the foles of time,
  Which die for goodnes, who haue liu'd for crime.

Here we find Shakespeare contrasting the strong, sure
structure of his love for his friend with the pitiful in-
security of some prince, some 'child of state' subject to

'accident,' who 'suffers in smiling pomp' and 'falls under the blow of thralled discontent.'

Very little familiarity with the momentous events of Shakespeare's times is required to recognize the ruler he is thinking of. A prince who, suffering shameful deprivation of his royal power, had with smiles dissembled his fierce resentment. A prince who, after waiting his time, deftly murdering his two capital enemies and reporting his deliverance to his politic Queen Mother, himself fell under the blow of an assassin who thought him a tyrant. This 'fortune's bastard,' this victim of 'time's hate,' is Henry of Valois, King Henri III of France, favourite child of Catherine de' Medici, and sometime suitor for Elizabeth's hand.

The first great 'accident' or misfortune that befell him was Paris's famous Day of Barricades, May 12, 1588, which the Venetian ambassador in Madrid called '*l'accidente di Francia contra quel povero Re*'—the accident of France against that poor King. On that day the people of Paris rose against their King in support of his enemies the Duke of Guise and the Holy Leaguers, who already had strong foreign backing in Pope Sixtus and Philip of Spain. Escaping immediate deposition by a hair's breadth, Henry managed to get away. He was obliged, however, to convoke the hostile States General, which sat throughout the autumn scorning him as a do-nothing king, and preparing to make their 'Caesar,' the Duke of Guise, master of the throne.

Elizabeth's ambassador to Henry, Sir Edward Stafford, describes for his Queen how her former suitor suffered in smiling pomp and hid his hate in affability. Stafford writes that though Henry 'was enforced to sett a faire face on the matter, and wisely to dissemble,' he 'laye hoovering in the winde to take the Duke and his fellow-conspirators at an advantage, when he might safelie . . . be revenged upon their cursed bodies.' Hearing that Guise intended to kill him on the approaching Christmas Eve, 1588, 'yett did the King make outward semblance as if he had suspected nothing,' but sat up all night scheming how to end his suffering by taking arms against a sea of troubles. Morning found him resolved to prevent his own murder 'if he could, by hazarding to kill the Duke the next daie.'[1]

In an earlier dispatch Stafford had sent off the first news of Henry's successful murder of the Duke, with his belief —later confirmed—that Guise's brother, the Cardinal of Lorraine, was also killed: Guise, he reports,

> was slaine by 8 of the *quarante cinq* who were there appointed for the same purpose; who executed theire charge so promptly as after he was entred into the said antechamber, hee neuer spake word vntill he was dead. The King beeing assured that hee was dead, and hauing seene him on the ground, hee went to his mother and told her, Madame I am now come to tell you that I am King without companion, and that the Duke of Guise, th'enemy of all my proceedinges, is dispatched.[2]

For his English theatre audience, Christopher Marlowe developed this scene of Henry viewing his dead enemy:

Captaine. My Lord, see where the Guise is slaine.
King. Ah this sweet sight is phisick to my soule . . .
  I nere was King of France vntill this houre:
  This is the traitor that hath spent my golde
  In making forraine warres and ciuile broiles.

---

[1] B.M. MS. Harley 4888 ff 9–25.
[2] B.M. MS. Cotton Galba D3/321.

Did he not draw a sorte of English priestes
From Doway to the Seminary at Remes,
To hatch forth treason gainst their naturall
    Queene?
Did he not cause the King of Spaines huge fleete
To threaten England and to menace me? . . .
Tush, to be short, he meant to make me Munke,
Or else to murder me, and so be King . . .
Nere was there King of France so yoakt as I.
The Massacre at Paris.

A few months later, in August 1589, the news was that
'Blood hath bought blood and blowes haue answerd
blowes.' As a contemporary partisan historian tells it,

a diuellish Monke, an excrement of hell, a *Iacobin* by
profession, *Iames Clement*, . . . vowes (said he) to kill
the Tyrant, and to deliuer the Cittie beseeged by
Sennacherib. . . . The King bends his eare, but instead of
hearing what he expected, this wretch drawes a knife
out of his sleeue made of purpose, thrusts his Maiesty
into the botome of the belly, and there leaues the knife
in the wound.

Or, as Marlowe has it in his play,

King. Ile read them Frier, and then Ile answere thee.
Frier. *Sancte Iacobus*, now haue mercye vpon me.
  He stabs the King with a knife as he readeth the letter . .

This brings us back to Shakespeare's line, *falls Vnder the
blow of thralled discontent*; and we can now consider the
background of the sonnet as a whole.

News of political assassinations has come thick and fast
across the Channel to England. Not long ago Henry of
France murdered the uncles of Mary Queen of Scots, the

THE MURDER OF HENRI III   Contemporary print, 1589

Duke of Guise and the Cardinal of Lorraine. Now we hear that a disgruntled friar, a partisan of the League, has murdered the King. 'Slaying is the word; it is a deed in fashion.' It makes us wonder whether English traitors may not take to king-killing in the French style, *whereto th'inuiting time our fashion calls.*

Shakespeare's theme in this sonnet is the grand impregnability of his love. Like some great and wise monarch of the forest, it fears no attack. Its growth is neither cheered by warmth nor checked by floods. But the contrasting image with which he began—some insecure prince such as the wretched fallen Henry of France, lightly plucked from life like a weed or flower—inevitably conjures up as its opposite the strong majestic figure of his English Queen, untouched by the many attempts on her life. He fuses the thought of her with the poetic image of his love. Any crafty assaults upon his love are to be scorned: they are as futile and fatuous as the short-laid, Jesuit-inspired plots to cut down Elizabeth. *To this I witnes call the foles of time, Which die for goodnes, who haue liu'd for crime.* These fools of time, who on the scaffold say they committed treason for religion's or conscience' sake, recall the young gentlemen of the recent Babington Plot to kill the Queen. Their folly and crime are repeatedly censured in contemporary books:

> ... him they schoole,
> And then transport to *England*, thear to play the dangerous Foole:
> Seducingly insisting on performance of their vow,
> That doth Rebellion, Regicide, and breach of Othes allow.

William Warner, *Albions England*, Bk. ix.

Barnwell . . . died an obstinate Papist and for his treason made conscience his best excuse. He had had but a rotten conscience that was infected with the murther of a vertuous Queene.

George Whetstone, *The Censure of a Loyall Subiect upon . . . those 14 notable Traitors*, 1587.

But these fond youthes (as wayward Children) did
Despise the counsell of their carefull Nurse,
And for the same they seeke her death . . .
These moued were for sacred *Conscience* sake
To do these deedes (a *Deuill* sure they were).
James Aske, *Elizabetha Triumphans*, 1588.

IV. CONCLUSIONS

So much for the more obvious allusions we have discovered in Sonnets 107, 123, and 124. Against the modern subjective criticism which treats these sonnets as difficult or obscure, John Benson's opinion in 1640 that they will be found clear and plain stands vindicated by the simple expedient of looking into the leading events of Shakespeare's Europe.

'The great poet,' remarks Mr. T. S. Eliot, 'in writing himself, writes his time.' If Shakespeare, the Soul of the Age, writes his time, his meanings are not hidden from his contemporaries. To them, his *Moone* is more than a poetic figure: it is an accurate and familiar description of the Armada's battle-formation. And this *Moone* was literally *mortall* or deadly. It killed a hundred Englishmen, and it meant to kill thousands more. To them, again, *pyramyds* is not metaphor for 'any modern marvels of architecture,' but the common name for certain particular and world-famous obelisks being set up by Pope Sixtus in Rome. Finally, for them there is no vagueness or generality about *the childe of state* who *suffers in smilinge pomp* and *falls Vnder the blow of thralled discontent*. This is plainly and exclusively the murdered Henry of Valois, King of France.

As for the date of these sonnets, we have seen that the *mortall Moone* was written in 1589, after the close of the Wonderful Year. The *pyramyds* sonnet, 1587–9, most probably in 1589. *The blow of thralled discontent* puts Sonnet 124 in 1589, after the beginning of August.

What do these discoveries reveal about the date of the rest of the Sonnets? In the 1609 arrangement as printed by Thomas Thorpe, these three all stand near the close of the 'first series' of 126 sonnets. And most of the proposed re-arrangements likewise regard them as belonging near the end of the group.

Here is a fact of cardinal importance. It indicates that *Shakespeare completed this main group of his sonnets by 1589.*

The evidence has led us to a revolutionary conclusion. Heretofore, theory has put the completion of the Sonnets anywhere from 1596 to 1603—from Shakespeare's thirty-third to his fortieth year. To realize the implications of placing his later sonnets as early as 1589—this will demand heroic efforts in casting off notions of Shakespeare long and fondly held.

The grand point which now rises to dwarf all else is the new knowledge—since the Sonnets unquestionably embody some of his highest poetry—that *Shakespeare's power had reached maturity by the time he was no more than twenty-five years old*. Yet strictly speaking he was still a beginner. Now at length we see that he is quite literal in writing in Sonnet 16 of his 'pupil pen.' Like Keats, Shakespeare sprang to maturity in his youth. Had Logan Pearsall Smith known the true date of the Sonnets, he would never have been forced by the mannered narrative poems to conclude that 'of all that wealth of poetic emotion seeking to find expression, that mass of brooding thought we are aware of in young poets like Shelley and Keats, there is no trace.' He would certainly have discovered a profusion of it in the Sonnets, which we may now study as an eloquent portrait of the artist as a young man: a young man expressing in his own person the very movements of the soul and the height of feeling which were later to appear in his plays.

We have long imagined that Shakespeare 'followed the vogue of sonnet-writing.' Rounding out a series of sonnets as a young man in 1589, we find him on the contrary setting rather than following the fashion; and outdoing the lamented leader, Sir Philip Sidney.

Other carefully fabricated structures of theory about Shakespeare's development as a poet must now be drastically altered. For example, *Venus and Adonis* and *Lucrece* were published in 1593 and 1594, and one of the articles of Shakespearean faith has been that they are 'more youthful work' than the Sonnets. What shall we say now?

One need not adopt Hazlitt's description of these two narrative poems as a 'couple of ice-houses' to recognize their striking inferiority to the profound and masterly work Shakespeare had already achieved four or five years earlier in his unpublished 'Sonnets among his private friends.' But how to account for it? The answer must lie in the sort of market for which they were prepared. *Venus* and *Lucrece* were the very stuff required to please the sophisticated taste of the wealthy patron to whom they were offered: that vain, fantastical, amorous, and hare-brained young sprout of the New Nobility, Southampton. As such they were a notable success; for the enthusiastic Gullios of the age exclaimed, 'Let this duncified worlde esteeme of Spencer and Chaucer, I'le worshipp sweet Mr. Shakspeare, and to honoure him will lay his Venus and Adonis under my pillowe.' But to peer into them for guide-posts to Shakespeare's 'development' is to look for what is not there.

And the poet's fair friend? What have our discoveries done with him? In Sonnet 104 Shakespeare tells us that he has known him for three years. If that disclosure belongs to 1589, the acquaintance was formed in 1586, when the poet was twenty-two. We may now assume that he had already begun his stage career by that date. And the marvellous poetic accomplishment growing out of the young player's friendship with 'W. H.' at last gives us work of the highest importance to put into the so-called 'lost years' of his life between 1585 and 1592.

As for the Dark Lady, we can now put her back where she belongs—with the mistresses of Jack Donne—in the poet's youth.

What must we now say of the noble candidates who have so long been pushed forward for the role of the young friend, 'Mr. W. H.'—the Earls of Pembroke and of Southampton? In 1586 Pembroke was, alas, but six years old. Under the circumstances he may be allowed to withdraw. And as for Southampton, late in the same year he began his second academic year at Cambridge and achieved his thirteenth birthday. This would make him all of sixteen when Shakespeare was finishing his Sonnets. Hardly as yet a man who has 'pass'd by the ambush of young days,' or one who at the outset of the Sonnets must be urged to marry and beget a son before it is too late. It looks as though we should have to give up Southampton too.

This is a welcome relief. How could anyone seriously expect us to believe that the publisher's dedication of 1609 to 'the onlie begetter of these insuing sonnets' as '*Mr. W. H.*' could possibly be taken as addressed to a right honourable peer of the realm? Not even a left-wing publisher of today would be guilty of so glaring a breach of manners. And for a Jacobean publisher, seeking a gift of money from the dedicatee,—utterly unthinkable. It is high time to lay away the Cinderella story about Shakespeare's imaginary intimacies with the nobility. To tell the truth, it was an ignorant fancy gotten by Bardolater out of Snobbery.

With the earls cleared away, we perhaps begin to see that if 'Mr. W. H.' means anything, it means what it undoubtedly meant in 1609: a gentleman or an esquire with those initials, generally known as the friend of Shakespeare who as a youth some twenty-odd years earlier inspired the writing of the Sonnets. Need I add that I am grooming a candidate for this position? But to propose him here would be premature and would make a tale too long for these pages.

LOVE'S LABOUR'S WON

'*Shakespeare* among the English is the most excellent in
both kinds for the stage; for Comedy, witnes his *Gentlemen of
Verona*, his *Errors*, his *Loue labors lost*, his *Loue labours wonne*,
his *Midsummers night dreame*, & his *Merchant of Venice* . . .'

No matter how many times we have heard this
passage from the *Palladis Tamia* ('Pallas's House-
keeper') of Francis Meres, published in 1598, we are still
baffled by the title which follows *Loue labors lost*: 'his
Loue labours wonne.' To what comedy does it belong?
For it will not do to imagine—because we have not been
able confidently to fit this title to a known play—that
somehow one of the six comedies rated by Meres as 'excellent' has been lost. Heminges and Condell, who carefully gathered and fostered their fellow Shakespeare's
'Orphanes,' declare that 'his wit can no more lie hid, then
it could be lost.' Certainly if a piece well known in 1598
and celebrated by Meres had been missing from their
collection of 1623, voices would promptly have been
raised in protest. No. It is generally agreed that we must
start with the premise that the play exists. And we should
also allow that whatever of mystery we find in the title is
of our own making. To Meres and his readers of 1598
there was no problem at all. In *Loue labours wonne* they
recognized an excellent comedy by Shakespeare.

Yet to the simple question '*which* of the known comedies is it?' our replies have been uncertain and various. At
present the favourite in the competition of guess-work
appears to be *All's Well that Ends Well*, with *The Taming*

of the Shrew a rather poor second. Sir Edmund Chambers points out that we have 'little to go upon, except the implications of the title itself, and the possibility of finding a play of early date not otherwise named by Meres.' With this we can all agree. But when Sir Edmund proceeds to say of *Loue labours wonne* that 'almost any love comedy might bear the title in question,' I cannot follow him.

A consideration of what the title implies makes it clear to me, first, that *Love Labours Won*—or *Love's Labours Won*, or *Love's Labour's Won*—cannot possibly refer to any one of the comedies which have been conjecturally suggested for the title; and secondly, that there is one, and only one, of Shakespeare's other comedies which fits the title, and that it fits like a glove to a hand.

To pass in review the conjectural proposals for *Love's Labour's Won* (for no doubt this form of the title is the correct one) is to see that all of them rely on the assumption that the title means 'Love's Difficulty is Overcome' or 'Love's Task is Achieved,' or something of the kind. Yet this presumed meaning of the phrase is without precedent or example in Shakespeare, and I do not find it anywhere in English. It should hardly be necessary to point out that in any language a labour (in the sense of a task) is properly said to be completed, performed, done, achieved, or accomplished; not *won*. A difficulty is conquered, overcome, or surmounted; not *won*. In this connection what *is* won is properly not the labour or task, but the reward for or the object of the toil: the wages, the prize, or the end, the goal. Is it not mere loose thinking and bad English to speak of a labour (in the sense of a task or difficulty) as *won* or *gained*?

The solecism is, however, demonstrably our own, and

not Shakespeare's. In the phrase *Love's Labour's Won* he is not talking of difficulties or tasks. His 'labour' in this instance is to be taken in the sense of Milton's 'sorrows and labours'—the Latin *aerumna*: 'sorrow, grief, trouble, painful labour, perplexing care, misery, affliction.' And what he means by 'winning love's labour' Shakespeare makes unmistakably clear in *The Two Gentlemen of Verona*, 1.1.32. Enumerating the miseries of being in love, Valentine says, 'If [*understood*, the object of love be] lost, why then a grievous labour won.' There is no mistaking the sense of *grievous labour*. It means *le chagrin d'amour*; and *won* means gained, obtained, or earned.

In the use of this locution Shakespeare is, of course, not peculiar. The notion of winning, earning, or gaining care, labour, sorrow, or grief in love is an Elizabethan commonplace. The ninth song in Dowland's *Second Book* (1600) has the following: *Reward for loue are labours for his paines.* Two passages from Greene's poems run: *Is that sweete That yeildeth sorrow for a gaine?* and *The gaine is greife to those that traffique loue.*[1] 'T.L.' (Thomas Lodge) thrice makes similar complaint of the unhappy winnings in the service of Love: *He vowes content, he paies with smart; Your Tropheis are annoyes*; and *He will repay me with annoy, Because a God.*[2] In the twenty-first of Thomas Morley's *Canzonets* (1593) we are told that *Love . . . slilie gaines cares passing great.* Henry Willoughby (schoolfellow and friend of Shakespeare's Thomas Russell) introduces Shakespeare himself into his *Avisa* (1594) as 'W.S. the old player,' and repeatedly

---

[1] Collins's Greene, ii. 250, 294.

[2] *The Phoenix Nest*, ed. H. E. Rollins, 54, 49; *Rosalynde*, ed. W. W. Greg, 28.

complains of gaining grief and pain in his hapless suit: *In curelesse care shall I alone Consume with griefe, that yields me gaine? . . Shall griefe rebound, where joyes grew? Of faithfull hart is this the gaine? . . . They do but frutelesse paine procure To haggard kytes that cast the lure.* Spenser (*F.Q.*, 1.5.43) uses a similar phrase of the trouble which a physician's great skill gains him. Night beseeches Æsculapius, *shew thy famous might In medicine, that else hath to thee wonne Great paines.* And Shakespeare's deposed king (*Rich. II*, 4.1.197) tells his supplanter Bolingbroke, *Your Care, is gaine of Care, by new Care wonne.*

Contrary, then, to what we have thoughtlessly assumed, to win labour in love, or to win Love's labour, is to earn or gain trouble, unhappiness, or grief. On consulting the Elizabethans, who were not so slipshod in their use of language as we are, it becomes evident that Shakespeare's *Love's Labour's Won* means no more and no less than *Love's Sorrow is Gained*. The title therefore points not to some member of the throng of love comedies where in a happy ending Jack hath Jill and naught goeth ill, but directly away to the lonely corner of the one comedy of lost love, where love's labour or pain is won. That comedy is, of course, *Troilus and Cressida*.[1] In calling it *Love's Labour's Won*, Shakespeare laid no claim to originality. For Chaucer at the close of his masterpiece had long before given him the hint for his title in pointing to the 'penaunce' and 'cares colde' gained by Troilus in

---

[1] I trust we may be spared the ingenious suggestion that *The Merry Wives* (which I have shown reason for placing in 1597) is *Love's Labour's Won*: that we be not invited to discover 'Love's labour' in the ducking, cudgelling, and to-pinching of the outwitted schemer, whose punishment is fittingly inflicted to the tune of *Fie on lust and luxury!*

his 'double sorwe': 'Lo here the fyn and guerdon for travaille . . . !'

The conclusion, indeed, seems both obvious and inevitable, once it is realized how the ironic force of 'winning Love's labour' has universally escaped us in modern times. We can now, however, hardly persist, against common sense and against idiom, and without authority, in trying to make *Labour's Won* mean something like *Task's Accomplished* or *Difficulty's Overcome*; especially if we can shake off our preconceptions and bring ourselves to pay attention to Chaucer, to the common practice of Elizabethan poets, and to the inescapable authority of Shakespeare's own illustration of the meaning of his phrase: 'If lost, why then a grievous labour won.' Or, to put it in another way, if anyone will now seriously assert that Shakespeare's 'labour's won' does *not* mean what Shakespeare shows it to mean, he must be invited to produce some other grammatical and idiomatic meaning for the phrase, and give authority and example for it.

In review, the titles *Love's Labour's Lost* and *Love's Labour's Won* are seen to be, like the plays themselves, linked, associated, neither parallel nor set in opposition to each other. The opposite of *Love's Labour's Lost* would obviously not be *Love's Labour's Won*, but *Love's Labour's Rewarded*. By both 'labour's lost' and 'labour's rewarded' we mean that *effort* has been expended—without return in the former, and with return in the latter. In the phrase 'labour's won,' on the other hand, 'labour' cannot mean *effort*, since one cannot 'win' or 'gain' an *effort*. As Shakespeare shows, it is 'labour' in the sense of trouble or sorrow which is gained or won in unhappy love.

41

As there is no opposition between the titles, neither is there parallelism; for 'labour' in the first title means 'effort,' while in the second it means 'sorrow' or 'pain.' Again they cannot be parallels, since Shakespeare drew them from two common proverbial phrases quite distinct in sense and tone, whose meanings and associations he could not alter if he would: the former is from the straightforward 'it is but labour lost' or 'you have lost your labour,' implying that your effort is wasted or in vain; the latter is from the ironic 'you have (gained) your labour for your pains' or 'you have your labour for your travail,' meaning that your bitter reward or winning for your effort is your pain, labour, or care. We may compare the complaint of Pandarus in this very play, 'I have had my labour for my travail.' In *Cymbeline* we have Pisanio's malediction of Cloten in his wicked pursuit of Imogen, 'Labour be his meed!' meaning 'May his pay be labour won!' or 'May he win labour!' Under these two titles, then, linked by a specious similarity, and to a careless modern eye contrasted, Shakespeare pictures unsuccessful love under two aspects: the one as effort wasted, and the other as sorrow gained.

The effect of identifying *Love's Labour's Won* is of course to push back the date of *Troilus and Cressida* (generally supposed to be 1601–2 or even later) at least as far as the first half of 1598. This removes the play in its original form from any imagined connection with the so-called 'war of the theatres' and the 'purge' which the Cambridge students thought Shakespeare gave to Ben Jonson. The 'Prologue arm'd,' found prefixed to the Folio text, which evidently glances at the 1601 prologue of Jonson's *Poetaster*, is not in the Quarto of 1609; and in any case it has no necessary connection with the first production of *Troilus and Cressida*.

This early date, 1598, brings the play much closer in the chronology to *Love's Labour's Lost*, which Chambers dates about 1595, and Professor Rupert Taylor 1596. Indeed, now that we see that Shakespeare linked the two comedies together by their similar names, it is hard to believe that more than a couple of years could have come between them; possibly they were closer still. With *Love's Labour's Won* identified as *Troilus and Cressida*, it is now clear that Francis Meres had reasons beyond their similarly proverbial titles for associating the two *Love's Labour* comedies. Both pieces are set off from the usual, popular, and somewhat hackneyed comedy form by 'unhappy' endings: the one unhappy in jest, the other in sober earnest. Both are highly 'intellectual,' witty, argumentative, and satirical, and patently aimed at a select, academic audience.

London's academic audience would, of course, be found in the 'four famous and renowned Colleges' of the law known as the Inns of Court. Together with the two Serjeants' Inns for serjeants and judges, they made up the 'most famous University for profession of Law, that is in the world,' and were attended and adorned by the social and intellectual *élite* of England. The acting of *The Comedy of Errors* at Gray's Inn and of *Twelfth Night* at the Middle Temple shows that attending to Shakespeare's comedies was regarded at these 'sumptuous, gallant, and rare nurseries for young students' as one of the 'commendable exercises fit for Gentlemen.'

For the sake of opening a fresh line of investigation, and since we are assured that *Troilus and Cressida* was 'neuer stal'd with the Stage, neuer clapper-clawd with the palmes of the vulger,' let us broaden the hypothesis of Professor Peter Alexander,[1] and suggest that *both* these '*Love's Labour*' comedies were prepared in the first instance for the entertainment of one of the law societies; and to make it specific, let us say for the revels of the Middle Temple, and see what can be brought up to support the conjecture.

As straws in the wind, we may note that Meres dedicated the work in which he writes so enthusiastically of Shakespeare to Thomas Eliot of the Middle Temple, Esquire (later Sir Thomas Eliot of Newlands, near Writtle, Essex). And the translator of Montemayor's *Diana*, on which Shakespeare based his *Two Gentlemen of Verona*, was Bartholomew Yonge of the Middle Temple, Gent. There proves to be a strong antecedent probability that Shakespeare had a special interest in the Middle Temple, and the Middle Temple in him. On looking into the matter, we find that among the gentlemen from what we now call the Shakespeare country who continued their education in London, the Middle Temple was the favourite Inn of Court. Even a rapid glance through the lists of admissions roughly covering his lifetime immediately yields forty or more from Shakespeare's neighbourhood.

Starting with those leaders of the Middle Temple with whom he had closest connections, we recall that of the Combe family. William Combe, M.P., of Warwick, Stratford, and London (allied to Quiney, Hales, and Sheldon) rose to the degree of Bencher and Reader of the Middle Temple. Late in his life Combe's chamber at the Inn was

---

[1] *Shakespeare's Life and Art* (1939), p. 195. *Troilus*, it is suggested, was written for performance at one of the Inns of Court.

taken over by his great-nephews, Shakespeare's neighbours and friends, William and Thomas Combe. Shakespeare's cousin and contemporary Thomas Greene of
Warwick rose even higher in the Middle Temple than the
elder William Combe, being chosen Treasurer in 1629.
On his admission in 1595, Greene's sureties had been the
Bencher John Marston of Coventry (formerly servant of
Lodowick Greville) and his son John Marston, later the
poet and playwright.

The roll of Middle Templars in Shakespeare's time
from the neighbourhood of Stratford is an impressive one,
and includes most of the leading gentry: William Catesby
of Ashby St. Legers, Lapworth, and Stratford; Richard
Woodward of Shottery Farm, Stratford; Lodowick
Greville of Milcote; Fulke Greville later Lord Brooke;
Henry Rainsford of Clifford Chambers and his step-
father William Barnes of Stratford; Thomas Grant and
Thomas Hales of Snitterfield; Edward Fisher of Warwick; Leonard Kempson of Arden's Grafton; Henry
Goodere of Polesworth; William Davies, Michael Rut-
ter, and Nicholas Overbury of Quinton; Edward Bushell
of Broad Marston; as well as Ingram of Wolford, Gibbes
of Honington, Throckmorton of Haseley, Skinner of
Rowington, Beaufoe of Guy's Cliffe, Edgiock of Ipsley,
Boughton of Lawford, Burgoyne of Wroxall, Somer-
ville of Edreston, Lee of Newnham, Ferrers of Baddesley,
Askew of Lapworth, Ward of Barford, Digby of Coles-
hull, Berry of Barton, and Verney of Compton Verney.
The list might be extended, but we need not labour the
point. The Middle Temple also claimed the family of
Shakespeare's intimate friend Thomas Russell: his
brother Maurice Berkeley (later M.P., member of the Vir-

ginia Council, and father of the playwright and governor of Virginia), his nephew Thomas Russell, and his step-father's cousin Charles Blount, later Earl of Devonshire, were all members of the society.

With this nexus in mind, let us return to the perform-ance in or before 1598 of *Troilus and Cressida* as *Love's Labour's Won*—which, with twenty-four parts for men and four for boy-actresses, was evidently prepared not for Shakespeare's company but for a large group of able amateurs—and examine other indications that may point to the Middle Temple. First there is the well-known piti-ful doggerel, chaffing both Shakespeare and the play, which Marston wrote into the *Histriomastix* of the fol-lowing year:

> Come Cressida, my Cresset light,
> Thy face doth shine both day and night;
> Behold, behold thy garter blue
> [Which emblem of his love so true][1]
>
> Thy knight [?on's] valiant elbow wears,
> That when he shakes his furious Speare
> The foe in shivering fearful sort
> May lay him down in death to snort.

This feeble satire on the actors, *Histriomastix*, was vamped up (let us charitably suppose, in haste) by John Marston of the Middle Temple, Shakespeare's country-man and bondsman of his cousin Thomas Greene. Sir Edmund Chambers is surely right in taking it to be an academic play—the parade of learning and the enormous number of characters indicate as much. But for what academy? I should go further, and suggest that Marston

---

[1] I have ventured to supply something here, as a line has evidently dropped out.

46

worked it up for his fellow-members of the Middle Temple to act. In that case the doggerel jests on Troilus and Cressida and on Shakespeare would be in place as topical hits on their own performance of the preceding year. And, we may add, the *Troilus and Cressida* for which Henslowe paid Dekker and Chettle in April 1599 would be the attempt of the Admiral's company to rival Shakespeare's play, just as their *Sir John Oldcastle* later in the same year was their clumsy reply to his *Henry IV.*

From another standpoint also, likelihood seems to lead us directly to the Middle Temple. The great wits Richard Martin and John Hoskins—later Ben Jonson's friends and leading members of the Mermaid and Mitre clubs— were both prime movers of the revels of the Middle Temple. As early as 1592 Martin had been expelled for four months as a ringleader in a rebellious lord-of-misrule frolic at the Inn's 'grand day' of Candlemas. And we know that he had already been enthroned as Prince d'Amour, attended by Hoskins as Clerk of his Privy Council and the Knights of the Quiver, when the honourable subjects of his Kingdom of Love danced their appropriately named *Masque of the Passions* at Court on Twelfth Night early in 1598. Martin wielded the royal sceptre of Love over the Middle Temple until he died, when his friend Hugh Holland (also Shakespeare's eulogist) mourned him in verse as *Princeps amorum, principum nec non amor*—The Prince of loves, and also the love of princes.

What then is more likely than that Dick Martin, seconded by Shakespeare's friends of the Middle Temple's Kingdom of Love, should ask the leading poet of love to give them plays for their grand nights, and that he should

respond with *Love's Labour's Lost* and *Love's Labour's Won*
—plays which precisely hit the vein of witty, *blasé* gentle-
men-students: satirical young men who scorn the senti-
mentality and the happy endings so dear to the vulgar?
For their subsequent Candlemas feast of 1602 they had
his *Twelfth Night*, which from its very beginning, 'If
music be the food of Love, play on,' aims the shafts of
comedy at the self-deluded fools of Love.

At this point it may not be out of place to throw in a
sample of Middle Temple holiday wit which I have found
produced by Dick Martin's successor on the throne of
Love: about 1635–6, when his highness entertained Prince
Charles Lewis of the Palatinate with Davenant's *Triumphs
of the Prince D'Amour, a Masque presented by his highness
at his Palace in the Middle Temple*. These were the decrees
promulgated under the title 'Certayne Edicts made &
published by ye commaund of ye right high & mighty
Prince, the Prince De l'Amour, to be observed & put in
execution by all his loveinge Subjects.' The argument will
not allow us to quote here much more than their headings:

An Edict ag^t the falce Dying of Love.

[That is, against dyeing love falsely as 'platonic'
love.]

An Edict against diffidence.

An Edict against retayling of Complements.

[Against 'exercising courtly phrases with certain
lewd women using about our Court commonly called Laundresses.']

An Edict against the Contumacy of Mistresses.

An Edict against Poets Adventurers.

We must, however, hear this last proclamation, since it
contains a new reference to Shakespeare:

AN EDICT AGAINST POETS ADVENTURERS

Having taken into our Princely consideration the
sundry abuses crept into our Court by reason of some
adventurous persons that haue throwne themselfes into the Thesp[ian] waters without any mannerly consideration or forthought whether they were formed fit
to touch it with the tip of their finger, wee being willing
to meet with s[uch] an enormity doe hereby declare
that noe person or persons whatsoever shall medd[le]
in Poetry for that they haue gathered with industry
phrases out of Shakespere Marston or the like or that
they thinke they haue a pretty vaine of lov[e wri]ting,
but only such as our privy Counsell shall find habile or
fitt for soe high Calling; wee being informed out of y^e
great M^r of Poetry Horace, that the[re] can be granted
noe such thing in nature as an indifferent Poet &
though one may be a good Lawyer or Physition,
though hee nether equall the king's Atturney or his
Doctour; yet it fares not soe in poetry it being granted
that n[o] mediocrity can serve a Poet; but that hee
must be excellent in his kind; Besides the late examples of some who ignorantly venturing upon this
Art, haue publickly demonstrated their want of grammatical skill, in joyning an Adjective Singular with a
Substantive Plurall, & another publishing a long quantity upon the stage for a short, through his want of
reading or advice before hand; & because by this
reason the Common wealth is not as well served as it
should be, for y^t he that is now against the will of all
the Muses a Poet might haue made a pretty Gentleman
Vsher, or an indifferent Courtier; we thinke it requisite
that every man apply himselfe to what he is fit for, &
leaue that which cannot become him, under paine
of having all his Collections confiscated to the use of
Chambermaids, waiting Gentlewomen & Barbers.[1]

---

[1] The full set of edicts will be found in Appendix C, p. 239.

It is at least amusing if not significant to find that the only two poets here named by the Prince de l'Amour are his own late subject, Marston, and Shakespeare, who as I suggest was the favourite dramatist of the Middle Templars. As for the mock edicts, I find them quite as necessary and salutary as the following two actual rules of the Elizabethan Middle Temple: 'None Irish men shall be admitted' and 'None shall eat oysters in the Hall.'

The other bit of new matter which may be injected at this point is a proposed identification of Dick Martin the Prince d'Amour (the friend and benefactor who saved Ben Jonson from prosecution in the Star Chamber) as the author of one set of commendatory verses prefixed to the published *Sejanus*, along with others by Marston and Hugh Holland. It includes the couplet

> For thou hast given each part so just a style
> That men suppose the action now on file—

a lawyer-like quibble on dramatic action and legal action —and is signed in Greek characters ΦΙΛΟΣ, which I take to be LOVE, the royal sign-manual of the learned Prince d'Amour, Dick Martin.

We now turn to examine the curious address to the Reader which appeared in some copies of the 1609 quarto of *Troilus and Cressida*, and which may have been written (though that is unlikely) as early as the 1603 entry of the book at Stationers' Hall. I suspect that this piece of wit and high appreciation of Shakespeare was the work perhaps of John Hoskins, or more probably of Dick Martin himself; and that its occasion was the release in 1609 to the common reader of this 'new play,' as the writer describes it, 'neuer stal'd with the Stage, neuer clapperclawd with the palmes of the vulger, and yet passing full of the palme comicall,' by its 'grand possessors': that is, as I believe, the gentlemen of the Middle Temple, whose chief times of studying the law were the 'grand vacations' in Lent and the 'grand vacations' in summer, and whose festivals besides Christmas were Candlemas, Ascension, S. John the Baptist, and Hallowmas, the four known as 'grand days.'[1] And if in your simplicity you were to object that the play belonged to its author, the legal brains of the 'grand possessors' would no doubt be ready to point out to you that the law recognizes at least 'three sorts of property, *viz.*, property absolute; property qualified (general and special); and property possessory.' They have hitherto retained *Troilus and Cressida* as property possessory (after all, it was written for them!), and have only now been prevailed upon to relinquish it for publication.

In several other particulars the address betrays its author as a lawyer-wit: its gentle girding at the grave magistrates as 'those grand censors' who (though they 'now stile them such vanities') would flock to hear Plays if they were called Pleas; its phrase 'at the perrill of your pleasures losse, and Iudgements'; and finally the observation 'by the grand possessors wills, I beleeve you should have prayd for them rather then beene prayd'—an obvious echo of the familiar and inevitable close of every petition to a magnate or complaint in equity to a judge: 'and

---

[1] It has been uncertainly conjectured that by the 'grand possessors' was meant Shakespeare's company, the King's men. But if (as I think) the author of the address was a barrister of the Middle Temple, it is impossible to see him referring even in irony to common players as 'grand.' Cuthbert Burbage's master, Sir Walter Cope, humorously classed the company with 'jugglers and such like creatures.'

your petitioner shall ever pray' or 'and your orator shall daily pray for the preservation of your good Lordship in honour long to continue.' By this the punning author no doubt implies that the 'grand possessors' would rather be sued unto as magnates or judges (who customarily are *prayd for* by humble beadsmen) than *pray* any common reader to buy a copy of *Troilus and Cressida.*

Another passage in the address sounds the authentic note of the Mermaid club:

> And all such dull and heavy-witted worldlings, as were never capable of the witte of a Commedie, comming by report of them to his [Shakespeare's] representations, have found that witte there, that they never found in themselves, and have parted better-wittied then they came; feeling an edge of witte set upon them, more then ever they dreamd they had braine to grinde it on.

Compare this with Frank Beaumont's nostalgic evocation, of about this same date, of the Mermaid feasts of wit:

> We left an Aire behind us, which alone
> Was able to make the two next Companies
> Right witty; though but downright fooles, more wise.

Looking back now at the first performance in 1598 of *Love's Labour's Won*, we can see how exactly it would fit the humour of the students of the law in their satirical court of the Prince of Love. The realistic-classical play of the love-lorn Troilus has hardly begun before Shakespeare, by a far-fetched figure about the process of making a cake, contrives to introduce a neat topical hit:

> *Pandarus.* . . . but you must tarry the bolting.
> *Troilus.* Have I not tarried?
> *Pandarus.* Ay, the bolting . . .

This seems peculiarly tame stuff unless we know that 'Bolting is a Term of Art used in our Inns of Court, whereby is intended a private arguing of Cases. . . . An Ancient and two Barristers sit as Judges, three Students bring each a Case, out of which the Judges chuse one to be argued; which done, the Students first argue it, and after them the Barristers. It is inferior to Mooting.' Every member of the audience, from 'inferior students' or 'slight puisnes' up, had been obliged to 'tarry the bolting.'

And as for mooting, who among the students of the law (which is a branch of ethical philosophy) could fail to recognize a shadow of that exercise—'the handling or arguing of a case'—in the ex parte disputations of Troilus, Paris, and Hector before the reverend Priam, who sets them the case: Shall we deliver up Helen? The various arguments are cogently presented; but the whole question is academic, as Hector shows. To keep Helen is now a matter of honour, and about that there can be no argument. Though for his relentless young audience Shakespeare strips this 'honour' to its essential skin of pride and vanity, it still shows far fairer than the black and base gangsterism of Achilles. For the rank Thersites, his general foul-mouthed railing seems to have hit the young gentleman's fashion of 1598. We find it again in that other Middle Temple production of the same year, Marston's Scourge of Villanie.

In providing the amateur players of the Middle Temple with Love's Labour's Won, Shakespeare gave them exactly the play they wanted. Troilus and Cressida would stretch their acting powers and display their learning in philosophy, their fire in passion. By its emphasis on degree and order it would not only underline the responsibility of their social position, but also, with Essex building up his power, would point to the dangers of 'hollow faction' and 'pale emulation.'[1] Better still, it was a play in which the cynical criticism and the disillusioned view of women, so dear to youthful sophisticates, could have their full swing. For them the marvellous mixture was neither comedy, tragedy, nor history: it was expression, it was life.

The earlier comedy, *Love's Labour's Lost*, probably acted for them by the professional company, reveals a lighter touch and a vein of satire more playful. No doubt the occasion was one to which ladies were invited. In tune with this lighter touch, we find Love's labour lost in a lyric of 1598 set by Giles Farnaby:

> The God of love came creeping
> Where Dians nimphs lay sleeping;
> He bent his bow, but mist his footing,
> And loosing, lost both labor, shaft, and shooting.

In this play too, produced 'when to be like the Court, was a playes praise,' we mark the topicality for a Court of a Prince of Love and his fellow gentlemen-scholars in the philosophy of the law, of a scene laid in the court of a prince whose book-mates and fellow-scholars have sworn to keep the statutes of their fellowship: to study and to see no women. Legal jests are thickly sown: 'intituled,

---

[1] The striking parallel—reinforced by the words of Chapman's 1598 dedication of his *Seven Books* to Essex as 'Achilles'—between the sulking of Achilles and the contemporary behaviour of Essex has been pointed out by Professor G. B. Harrison, whose inference is 'that *Troilus and Cressida* in its present form was performed privately before an anti-Essex audience, either in the summer of 1598, or else about two years later, when Essex and his followers were brewing treason.' *Times Literary Supplement*, Nov. 20, 1930.

nominated, or called,' 'taken with the manner,' and 'in manner and form following.' These have, of course, been remarked, but so far as I know Shakespeare's byplay on the form of an indictment for felony has passed unnoticed. In his *Symboleographie*, William West gives 'An order to be observed in the right framing of an Indictment [for theft]: "*Quis* [Who?] The person with his name, surname, addicion of the Towne, Countie, Arte, and degree. *Quando* [When?] The day and yeare. *Ubi* [Where?] The place, Towne, and Countrie. *Quid* [What?] The thing taken, the colour, the marke, the price and value. *Cuius* [Whose?] The owner of the thing and whose it was. *Quomodo* [How?] The manner of the doing and how. *Quare* [Why or wherefore?] The entent, which is comprised in this word (*Felonice*)." '

This meticulous legal rigmarole is deliciously hit off in Armado's letter to the King:

... The time When? About the sixth hour, when beasts most graze, birds best peck, and men sit down to that nourishment which is called supper. So much for the time When. Now for the ground Which? which, I mean, I walk'd upon. It is ycliped thy park. Then for the place Where? where, I mean, I did encounter that obscene and most prepost'rous event that draweth from my snow-white pen the ebon-coloured ink which here thou viewest, beholdest, surveyest, or seest. But for the place Where? It standeth north-north-east and by east from the west corner of thy curious-knotted garden. There did I see that low-spirited swain, that base minnow of thy mirth—
Costard. Me!

In conclusion, let me sum up in brief what I think I have found, together with the theory developed from it.

As Shakespeare tells us in *The Two Gentlemen of Verona*, *Love's Labour's Won* unquestionably means *Love's Sorrow is Gained*, and consequently it can be nothing else than the alternative title of *Troilus and Cressida*.

This discovery fixes the date of the first performance of *Troilus and Cressida* at least before the autumn of 1598.

Shakespeare's demonstrated connections with the Middle Temple, internal evidence in *Troilus and Cressida*, the doggerel jests in the academic *Histriomastix* of 1599 by Marston of the Middle Temple on 'Cressida' and 'shakes his furious Speare'—all these point to the conclusion that the play was made for the Middle Templars to act in 1598.

The address to the Reader in the quarto of 1609, releasing this private play for publication, was written by a lawyer-wit, no doubt Dick Martin of the Mermaid club himself, and is thoroughly consonant with the theory.

On its 'grand days' of revels the Middle Temple was the Kingdom of Love; and Shakespeare's linked plays *Love's Labour's Lost* and *Love's Labour's Won* by their titles, their tone, and their contents were pre-eminently suited for the witty entertainment of the 'grand possessors,' under the ironical sceptre of his royal highness Richard (Martin), Prince d'Amour.

COMPLACENCY is painfully dented every time one is forced to realize that it is not we moderns who are the able and qualified appreciators of Shakespeare. We do our best, but we enter the competition about three and a half centuries late. It is annoying to have to admit, for instance, that our Opposite Number in Shakespeare's audience must have got far more enjoyment out of him than we can. We could wish that Shakespeare were the soul of our age, as he was of his own; but he isn't. Nor is he—while yet maintaining a unique eminence—in our day the applause, delight, and wonder of the stage. Granting that the Sweet Swan of Avon enchanted Elizabeth and James, can he truthfully be said to bewitch Elizabeth and George? Small blame to us, then, if we regard our Elizabethan Opposite Number with a greenish eye. For the advantages were all his. His was the story; he belonged to the landscape, body and soul; the strings of his being were wound up to the key of the music: ear and mind took the full flood of overtones and associations direct, freely and easily, as a nook of the bay takes a spring tide. Happy man!

Instead of merely envying him, however, we might try asking him to lend us a hand, or at least to point out something obvious that we have missed. How are we to tell what the Elizabethans especially relished in Shakespeare? One evident guide to contemporary taste is presented by favourite, large-selling playbooks, and particularly by their title-pages. In those days, we are told, title-pages did additional duty as advertisements. Offprints of them were handed round and displayed to catch the buyer's eye. For this reason we find the publisher drawing on the attractive content of the book for an alluring title-page: *Tamburlaine the Great. Who, from a Scythian Shep-hearde, by his rare and woonderfull Conquests, became a most puissant and mightye Monarque. And (for his tyranny, and terrour in Warre) was tearmed, The Scourge of God. Deuided into two Tragicall Discourses* ... Shakespeare himself turns to this common practice for a simile:

> Yea, this man's brow, like to a title-leaf,
> Foretells the nature of a tragic volume.

Now, everybody knows that Falstaff on the stage was a smash hit. He not only stopped the show but also (O rare!) arrested the hungry and perpetual motion of the nut-chewing groundlings:

> I could ... tell how long
> Falstaff from cracking nuts hath kept the throng.

Naturally, the publisher of *Henry IV Part I* seized on this popularity to spread his name on the title-page. *The History of Henrie the Fourth* ... *With the humorous conceits of Sir Iohn Falstaffe*. In forty years this playbook went into at least eight editions. And every quarto of the two other pieces in which Falstaff figured gave his name a similar display.

Just here is where our Elizabethan playgoer jogs our elbow, and meaningly points to another favourite of his whom we have not known how to prize at the Elizabethan rate: Falstaff's follower, Ancient (Ensign) Pistol. For, observe, in every published play in which he appears with Falstaff, Pistol shares the billing with that sweet knight.

The Second part of Henrie the fourth . . . With the humours of sir Iohn Falstaffe, and swaggering Pistoll. . . . Syr Iohn Falstaffe, and the Merrie Wiues of Windsor . . . With the swaggering vaine of Auncient Pistoll, and Corporall Nym. And in *Henry V*, which reports the pathetic death of Falstaff, Pistol stands alone in the glare of publicity with the hero-king: *The Chronicle History of Henry the fift . . . Togither with Auntient Pistoll.*

Where, we ask, is Poins? Or Bardolph? Or Mistress Quickly? Where is Mr. Justice Silence? Or, for that matter, where is Captain Fluellen, whom Hazlitt ranks as the most entertaining character in *Henry V*? It is not they who make the front page, but Pistol. And the rascal makes it in every play he graces: three times, which ties with the record set by Falstaff, and easily distances all the other minor characters in Shakespeare. The evidence of Pistol's first-class popularity on the stage and in the book is inescapable. There must have been a reason for it.

But what has happened today? Falstaff (that varlet vile and base Phrygian Turk) has eclipsed his henchman. In the movie of *Henry V* the swaggering Ancient is reduced and deformed to a pitiful burlesque. It would not surprise me if Pistol, in disgust, a Mars of malcontents, should discharge himself of our company and go off somewhere else, where there are ears worthy to hear his thunderous report. Must we show ourselves unable to relish a character which delighted our forerunners, one which Shakespeare produced with evident gusto?

If not, where are we to look for the secret of Pistol's charm for the Elizabethans? His rascality alone will not give us the key, any more than the excesses and delinquencies of Falstaff will explain what makes us love that tun of man. And yet to the casual eye rascality would seem to be his long suit, since by those who handle him Pistol is double-charged with a heavy load of brimstone epithets. To call them over will give us a hint both of the reserves of Elizabethan vituperation and of the Pistolfan versatility in vileness which brought them into action.

To his various acquaintance Pistol is nine times a rogue, and, into the bargain, a mouldy rogue, and the foul-mouth'dst rogue in England. A rascal fourfold; and for good measure a swaggering rascal, a fustian rascal, a bottle-ale rascal, a cut-purse rascal, a cony-catching rascal, and an arrant counterfeit rascal. Further, he is twice a slave, and a rascal, bragging slave. He is likewise a cheater, a tame cheater, an abominable damned cheater, and a poor, base, rascally, cheating, lack-linen mate. To add to this, he is a scurvy, lousy knave twice over, thrice a scald knave; a counterfeit cowardly knave, a rascally, scald, beggarly, lousy, bragging knave; a cogging companion, a scurvy companion, and a fellow, look you now, of no merits. What is more, he is a bawd, a villain, a fool, and a gull; a basket-hilt stale juggler, a roaring devil (and coward), and a swasher. He is, finally, a cutpurse and a filthy bung; and, in sum, an unconfinable baseness and a slander of the age.

Beyond question we have here a lavish 'provant' of contempt, a general issue of infamy. The replenished rogue Pistol draws more than any other irregular in Shakespeare's band. And all of it, I should agree, deserved, with perhaps two or three exceptions. Captain Gower (who, it must be granted, doesn't know him very well) gives him, among other things, the titles of 'fool' and 'gull.' These must be received with caution. Cer-

tainly Pistol foolishly mistook his man when he insulted
Fluellen; but if he were a thoroughgoing fool and gull he
could hardly cut a figure as a cony-catcher, a cheater, or
a cutpurse and a bung. No doodle or cokes could qualify
for such arts, which exacted from even their humbler professors a modicum of forecast, of cunning and skill. As
for 'the foul-mouth'dst rogue in England,' this is one of
Mistress Dorothy Tearsheet's contributions, and from
her studies of rhetoric in 'the university of Bridewell' she
should be a judge; but in fairness it must be allowed that
what we hear of Pistol's speech is, with a few exceptions,
surprisingly clean.

It is clear enough that Pistol is treated by those who
know him best as unmitigated scum of the earth. Exhilarating though this is, it cannot alone account for his great
popularity. Nor can the swagger which covers his simon-
pure cowardice do it. Bobadill, Parolles, Bessus, and their
likes are also cowards good and true, but they lack some
rare quality which endeared Pistol to his public. Once
more, then, what is Pistol's charm?

I should say that his gift is a daemon possessing him
with the conviction that he is essentially a Locrine, a
Cambyses, a Tamburlaine. Not, of course, the insane
notion that he is a real tyrant king, but the wildly absurd
one that he is a *player king*. Thus he can rehearse valour
without requiring courage, carry tempest in his voice
without running any measurable risk. The fact that the
rascal wants to be a tragedy king is a hint of the high-
aspiring soul to be found even in the Turnbull Street of
Marlowe's London. 'A stage player, though he be but a
cobler by occupation, yet his chance may be to play the
King's part.' Pistol, however, scorns the base mind of a

Bottom, living in hope to be cast for Ercles. Hope is a curtal dog in some affairs, and Pistol has stormed his fortunes and cast himself.

Long ago his genius whispered him in the ear, 'Thy part is on the stage, for thou must bear the person of a King.' Since that memorable day he has been sustaining the role, unsupported, and against heavy odds, in a performance continuous, non-stop, round the clock. When he lacks an audience he magnificates *solus*, 'nor omitting ceremonies of bravery in the infamy of his nature.' What though need constrains him to turn bawd, or to filch a living with 'five-and-a-reach'? His parting soliloquy, issued from a head bloodied by the cudgel of a disillusioned and outraged Fluellen, reveals a spirit unbowed by Fortune's tortures vile—

Doth Fortune play the huswife with me now?

Though creeping Time is at his gate, and to regain his 'honour' after a public beating will call for a hero's effrontery, yet will he conquer, turning the badges of infamy into glorious wounds:

Old I do wax, and from my weary limbs
Honour is cudgell'd. . . .
And patches will I get unto these cudgell'd scars,
And swear I got them in the Gallia wars.

Pistol entered on his career of antic majesty with certain solid advantages; for Nature has seconded his aspirations. To begin with, she gave him a stalwart figure and a swelling, formidable carriage. Though attired in a 'horrid suit o' the camp,' a filthy military cassock, he wallows in his walk, his rags to grace, and looks as tall a man as ever opened oyster. He can cultivate a lion's mane, and

fur his face like a *soldado* with a spade beard, broad, pen-
dant, of the terrible cut, and mustachios like twisted
poniards. A mouth wide, to encompass his furious voci-
ferations; an eye now flashing like a catamount's, now
haughtily cast aloft 'as if he would quarrel with the moon,
or had some controversy with the seven stars.'

He has haunted the theatres and studied the great actors, mastering the threatening trick of Dunstan's brows
and the scenical strut of Alleyn's Cutlack-gait; practised
domineering, staring, facing and outfacing, stalking up
and down, and exclaiming with a terrible hollow voice:

> Base peasant, humbly watch my stately looks
> And yield applause to every word I speak,
> Or from my service I'll discard thee quite!

The experienced and witty Boy in *Henry V*—a well-edu-
cated infant who speaks French and used to serve Prince
Hal—knows that Pistol's reading of the part comes very
near to the character of the raging infernal tyrant, the
'roaring devil i' the old play.' In his calmer intervals Pistol is still in character: the kingly lion whose nature is too
noble to harm the silly sheep; and he addresses his walk-
ing-mates as 'lambkins.'

We first sight Ancient Pistol in an intimate scene at the
Boar's Head Tavern, where Falstaff is taking his ease and
his sherris sack with his Mistress Doll Tearsheet (who is
somewhat distempered with Canary), Hostess Quickly,
and Corporal Bardolph. By grossly assuming the insignia
of a captain, the Ancient has augmented his swagger.
Being also drunk, he so far forgets his 'pageant majesty'
as to neglect his disdainful and invariable style of thee,
thy, and thou, in a leering familiar equivoque on Doll:
'Then to *you*, Mistress Dorothy; I will charge *you*. . . . I

know *you*, Mistress Dorothy.' Fired with scorn and fury, Doll reaches for her knife; she is meat for his betters; and she overwhelms him with a torrent of the abuse he deserves. Pistol retorts with a deadly threat to murder her ruff and to tear her.

The others have had enough of a drunken Pistol, and they try to get him to go quietly. But rage has hoisted him once more on to his stuffed Pegasus, and 'he will make her know that Locrine can brook no braves.' 'I'll see her damn'd first! to Pluto's damnéd lake, by this hand, to th'infernal deep.' Doll? A toy! A packhorse, a Galloway nag, a pamper'd jade of Asia! Shall overridden trash like that compare with world-commanders such as Pistol, 'with Caesars, and with Cannibals, And Troyan Greeks? Nay, rather damn them with King Cerberus, and let the welkin roar!' And with that he bends his brows, and fetches his stations up and down the room 'with such furious gesture as if he had been playing Tamburlaine upon a stage.'

A little more, and, coward though he is, the actor's arrogance has him. His winish wits are superintoxicated with high astounding terms; he cannot heed the ominous change in Falstaff's tone; and the catastrophe of the raging ragamuffin is a degrading tumble down the stairs with a real rapier wound in his counterfeit-captain shoulder. How are the mighty fallen! But he brings down the house with him.

The other great histrionic set-to in the Pistol story is also over one of Falstaff's women: Hostess Quickly. After Sir John declines to make her his lady, Nell Quickly's romance is a devious one. Her fortune—the Boar's Head—attracts a humbler member of the gang, the shock-headed, drawling, darkly-hinting little Corporal Nym. Wasting no words, Nym carries the flutterbudget Quickly by storm, and 'makes her sure' by a troth-plight tantamount to marriage.

But alas for honour among thieves! In *The Merry Wives*, Pistol the pirate-king also picks up the scent of marriageable money, and to snatch Nell away from his friend he plunges after the prey like a fell Dunkirker:

Clap on more sails, pursue! Up with your fights! Give fire! She is my prize, or ocean whelm them all!

There is irony as well as thievery in the capture. The Quickly who'll have no swaggerers, who has not lived all this while to have swaggering now, who'll not have your ancient swaggerer come in her doors, who is the worse, and shakes an 'twere an aspen leaf when one says 'swagger'—this extreme swagger-phobe breaks her troth plighted to Nym to marry Pistol, the swaggerer most abominable. How did Pistol carry it off? If wily words will seduce witless woman, a man of his 'rare vocabularity' could easily supplant the laconic Nym. More than that, after his theatrical studies it would be no trick for him to work up a very specious passion. We may be sure that in unfolding the depth of his affections the Ancient framed his tongue (that was wont to sound nothing but threats of war) to utter a honey-sweet tale of love.

At all events, Pistol has played rob-thief, Nell Quickly is linked in wedlock with that 'lofty thrasonical huff-snuff,' and the damage is already done when in *Henry V* we meet the crew again. Bardolph, now promoted lieutenant, is troubled at the hostility which Pistol has kindled by his Rape of Helen-of-the-Boar's-Head. Menelaus-Nym, like Mars in his wrath, sitting upon his drum, devising tragedies of revenge, is full of suggestions dark and bloody: 'Men may sleep, and they may have their throats about them at that time; and some say knives have edges.' But Bardolph prefers peace to slit weasands; he will even 'bestow a breakfast' to make the two fell opposites friends once more.

Then comes the crisis, the imminent Trojan War, on the entrance of Ancient Pistol with his wedded booty. Bardolph vainly begs Nym to be patient. The next line, with its insult, 'How now, *mine host* Pistol?' is, of course, Nym's opening shot in the quarrel, and the Quarto version of *Henry V* assigns it to him. (The commonly followed Folio text—out of which the speech-prefix *Nym* has undoubtedly dropped—absurdly gives these fighting words to Bardolph the pacifier, making nonsense of the scene.) The shot goes home. Pistol is stung; but his retort rubs it into Nym with '*my* Nell,' and how he commands her:

> Base tyke, call'st thou me host?
> Now by this hand I swear I scorn the term.
> Nor shall my Nell keep lodgers.

As Quickly rattles on in her characteristic vein of unconscious bawdry, the two men suddenly draw; and in the flash of naked cutlery her prophetic soul already sees her new husband carved and useless: 'O welliday Lady, if he be not hewn now!'

What fetches the audience in the following scene is its superb make-believe. We know that 'their valours are not yet so combatant, or truly antagonistic as to fight,' because they have no valour. But they make their Paris–Menelaus quarrel over the peerless Helen Quickly, the 'only she,' *look* terrifically Trojan; and Bardolph plays up nobly, coming between the thundering Pistol and the snarling Nym as if there were actual danger of homicide:

Bard. Good Lieutenant—good Corporal—offer nothing here.

Nym. Pish!

Pist. Pish for thee, Iceland dog! thou prick-ear'd cur of Iceland!

Hostess. Good Corporal Nym, show thy valour, and put up your sword.

Nym. Will you shog off? I would have you solus.

Pist. 'Solus,' egregious dog? O viper vile!
　　The 'solus' in thy most mervailous face!
　　The 'solus' in thy teeth, and in thy throat,
　　And in thy hateful lungs, yea, in thy maw, perdy!
　　And, which is worse, within thy nasty mouth!
　　I do retort the 'solus' in thy bowels;
　　For I can take, and Pistol's cock is up,
　　And flashing fire will follow. . . .

Bard. Hear me, hear me what I say! He that strikes the first stroke, I'll run him up to the hilts, as I am a soldier.

Every word in this unparalleled scene is calculated, and bears upon the mighty argument—the Rape of Helen Quickly. Pistol retorts the hissing and the envious 'pish!' and strikes back with 'Iceland dog'—a triple sneer at Nym. The shag-haired, stupid, and waspish little Iceland cur was fancied for its sauciness and quarrelling. Nym's answering snarl dares Pistol to the single fight outside: 'Will you shog off? I would have you solus.' Solus? The word lashes Pistol into a fury. Why? Puzzled commentators have imagined some misunderstanding, or that Pistol (and he a man that can quote legal Latin!) doesn't know the meaning of the word. The truth is that he knows it only too well; he 'can take' Nym's viperous and double meaning at the full. For as well as 'single in the field,' solus also means *unmarried*. Nym would kill him and take his wife, leaving him not only dead but single too. Single? roars Pistol, passing his free arm momentarily round his Helen's portly middle. Single thyself! The 'single' in thy bachelor bowels!

Provided he can keep his plunder, Pistol is ready to make peace, if given half a chance. Bardolph valiantly offers the chance, but Nym still feels he ought to cut Pistol's throat at some convenient time. *Couple a gorge!* What, again? Never! All Troynovant shall topple, thou lying Cretan hound, ere Pistol to Nym's cuttle his windpipe will lay bare, or his Helen to the cloying clutch of Nym. Base slave, if thou must marry,

> . . . to the spital go,
> And from the powd'ring tub of infamy
> Fetch forth the lazar kite of Cressid's kind,
> Doll Tearsheet she by name, and her espouse.
> I have, and I will hold the quondam Quickly
> For the only she; and, pauca, there's enough.

Pistol's scorn and defiance are deftly deflated by the abrupt announcement that Falstaff is very sick at the Boar's Head and needs their help. Before Nym will be appeased, however, he saves a little face by forcing a promise out of Pistol to pay most of an eight-shilling debt. Trojan War is averted; Pistol grandly gives Nym his hand, and they are off to condole the stricken knight, whose rejection by a reformed King Harry has left his old heart 'fracted and corroborate.'

Their next scene, that of mourning the dead Falstaff, is as miraculous as anything in literature. Here Shakespeare coolly and easily performs the impossible. Without yielding an inch of the wild comedy characteristic of each of these humorists, he gives (to quote Mr. Kittredge) an effect of almost unendurable pathos. Shakespeare's boldness is as startling as his skill. In Quickly's tale of Falstaff's dying, he lets her not only muddle her words as usual but even keep to her vein of unconscious bawdry; and yet somehow the latent laughter does true sorrow no wrong.

But Pistol is our theme; and this scene is distinguished by one of his finest unappreciated touches, when he says:

No; for my manly heart doth yearn.
Bardolph, be blithe; Nym, rouse thy vaunting veins;
Boy, bristle thy courage up; for Falstaff he is dead,
And we must yearn therefore.

It has been assumed that Pistol here defies logic; that is, talks nonsense. To think so is to lose sight of what Pistol never forgets—his role as a tragedy-king. 'I mean myself still in the plural number.' Here is a Great Sorrow; and it takes a mighty heart to yearn heroically. These others—shallow subjects, poor narrow souls—are incapable of the passion. Let them (he mournfully intones, with large dismissive gestures) be blithe, and cheery, and careless, while we—the king—show Sorrow in her sable robes of tragedy. And with that he withdraws himself, strikes a solemn pose of woe, and remains majestically aloof and profoundly sunk until it is time to make a move.

Contrast intensifies the fun in his two next bits. Dropping the sable trappings, he turns lofty merchant-prince, laying prudent commercial maxims and enjoining Nell to 'look to my chattels and my moveables.' Another turn, and it is the stirring summons, 'Yoke fellows in arms, Let us to France'—like the warlike Harry himself, we think; when the sharking Pistol breaks through with a trigger-burst of frankness—'like horse-leeches, my boys, To suck, to suck, the very blood to suck!'

Then France, and Pistol at Harfleur. King Harry's thrilling call, 'Once more unto the breach!' has infected the fiery-nosed Bardolph; but his excited echo, 'On, on, on, on, on! to the breach! to the breach!' is coldly received by Nym and Pistol, who have no stomach for hot knocks. Even Fluellen, basting their reluctant rears with the flat of his sword, cannot beat them up to danger and duty. Their humour is for looting, which works the undoing of Nym and Bardolph. Both of them swing for it. Pistol alone proves durable. As the Boy observes, he would have been hanged too, 'if he durst steal anything adventurously,' but inexpugnable cowardice preserves him. Pistol, indeed, as one great leader to another, appeals to Fluellen to ask for Bardolph's reprieve:

> . . . let not Bardolph's vital thread be cut
> With edge of penny cord and vile reproach.
> Speak, Captain, for his life, and I will thee requite.

He takes Fluellen's refusal to intervene as a gross affront calling for revenge on the Welshman; and this theme is carried forward when Pistol has his 'little touch of Harry in the night.' Here we find the headliners, 'Henry the fift . . . Togither with Auntient Pistoll,' alone and face to face. Pageant majesty confronts true majesty in disguise:

> *Pist.* Discuss unto me, art thou officer?
> Or art thou base, common, and popular?
> *King.* I am a gentleman of a company. . . . What are you?
> *Pist.* As good a gentleman as the emperor.
> *King.* Then you are better than the king. . . .

Pist. Know'st thou Fluellen?

King. Yes.

Pist. Tell him I'll knock his leek about his pate
      Upon Saint Davy's day.

King. Do not you wear your dagger in your cap that day, lest he knock that about yours.

Pist. Art thou his friend?

King. And his kinsman too.

Pist. The *figo* for thee then!

King. I thank you. God be with you!

Pist. My name is Pistol call'd.

King. It sorts well with your fierceness.

Harry's amused prophecy is fulfilled; yet before the fatal moment for Pistol to be beaten to his knees and made to munch the nauseating leek he has insulted, the Ancient has two scenes of glory: the one written and the other indicated. In the one, he domineers frightfully over a terrified French captive, calling him a 'damnéd and luxurious mountain goat,' and threatening to 'fetch his rim out at his throat in drops of crimson blood.' To keep his throat uncut, this grovelling Monsieur le Fer offers heavy ransom, taking Pistol to be 'the most brave, valorous, and thrice-worthy signieur of England.' Ha! The French at least can recognize a Caesar, and a Cannibal, and a Troyan Greek when they see one. 'As I suck blood, I will some mercy show! Follow me, cur.' This is Pistol's grandest exit.

The other glorious scene is Pistol at the bridge. This Shakespeare wrote only by implication; Fluellen's brief report of it 'stands for the whole to be imaginéd.' If only we had Shakespeare's Pistol at the bridge written, as a foil to his Harry at the breach! Perhaps we should then see Captain Fluellen, and the rest of Exeter's command, toughly holding the bridge, spellbound, stirred, and exalted by Pistol's brazen tongue and his port 'like Mars approaching to a bloody field.' Like the stage-intoxicated cockney warriors who had embarked with Drake and Norris, these London lads had also been reluctantly forced to

> Bid theatres and proud tragedians,
> Bid Mahomet, Scipio, and mighty Tamburlaine,
> King Charlemagne, Tom Stukely and the rest
> Adieu.

Yet here at the front, in the thunderous and bloody Continental theatre of war, they find themselves drinking in a terrific blood-and-thunder one-man show. From a well-sheltered corner, Ancient Pistol—a Duke of Plaza-Toro, or a Goliath grown prudent—blows them mightily on to renown; rolling an eye more 'infestious' than the basilisk's upon the adversary, while he volleys forth his cannon braves with the deep-mouth'd roar of a huge full-chargéd culverin. Who shall say that a coward, if he but cheer tyrannically enough, cannot hearten brave men on the field? No reflection, of course, on the superb exhortation of the valorous King Harry. But to the hypnotized Welsh captain, the guttersnipe Pistol seemed as valiant a man as Mark Antony. For among the feats of valour 'committed at the pridge' he *saw* him 'do as gallant service.'

We cannot do Pistol justice (in view of this sincere tribute) without a word about his style. It is not enough to say that his lingo is largely catchwords and misquotations of resounding bits from old plays. Certainly the play particles are there, and often brought in with great aptness, but there is more to it than that. An integral part of his role is a conviction that 'nothing better becometh kings than literature.' His cloudy home is on Parnassus,

> Where Phoebus with the learned Ladies nine
> Delight themselves with music harmony.

Since verse is more choice and memorable, and far more effective in delivery than prose, with him it is

> Fetch me the robe that proud Apollo wears,
> That I may jet it in the capitol!

Where a lesser man might tell Falstaff, 'I will make good the amount in (stolen) clothes,' Pistol's exacting rhetorical standard demands, 'I will retort the sum in equipage.'

When he arrives swelling with the revolutionary announcement of the death of the old king, Pistol must hold his audience in suspense while he patrols the dazzling corridors of his airy castle:

> And tidings do I bring, and lucky joys,
> And golden times, and happy news of price.

Falstaff labours to make him come off, first with an appeal to reason, and then with ridicule, but the only result is a wounded poetic dignity:

> *Fal.* I pray thee now deliver them like a man of this
>   world.
> *Pist.* A *foutra* for the world and worldlings base!
>   I speak of Africa and golden joys.
> *Fal.* O base Assyrian knight, what is thy news?
>   Let King Cophetua know the truth thereof.
> *Silence.* (*sings*) And Robin Hood, Scarlet, and John.
> *Pist.* Shall dunghill curs confront the Helicons?
>   And shall good news be baffled?
>   Then, Pistol, lay thy head in Furies' lap!

Since Pistol is a 'Helicon,' a king of poets, or a poet-king, words are his stock-in-trade as well as his magic and his private glory. He employs them imperiously, if occasionally (like Humpty Dumpty) working them too hard. *Fracted* is a good Latinism, but when *corroborate* is teamed up with it, the result is an 'enigmatical epithet.' And now and then a word gets out of hand, as for instance *Cannibal* for *Hannibal,* or *Cerberus* for *Erebus.* But on the whole Pistol guides the chariot of Phoebus Old Style with a master's touch.

Of course, his lofty lines and his formal inversions of verse ('My name is Pistol call'd'), when absurdly pressed into scenes of realism, are taken as fustian by everyone. Yet without doubt they gave peculiar delight to an audience that at other times entered wholeheartedly into the rant of Tamburlaine: just as in our day only those who have taken melodrama seriously can fully enjoy a delicate satire on its style and conventions. And the spectacle of Pistol's verse-and-glory fixation, to an audience whose own brains were a trifle turned by a heady dose of high astounding terms, would release the best of all laughs— at the comedy of one's own human folly. For where does drama leave off and melodrama begin? Or where does poetry leave off and fustian begin? No critic can draw the line firmly except for himself; and even there his magisterial sounding-board may alter with knowledge, mood, or circumstance. To dismiss Pistol's fustian with contempt is to miss its point. It is his poetry; and who are we to say that it does not give him an authentic Housman thrill up the spine?

Hazlitt calls Pistol a caricature in the manner of Dickens. This description needs to be qualified. To be sure, his style of talking in verse is a caricature of the magniloquent stuffing of the huge bombastic plays. But Pistol himself is rather what Ben Jonson might call a creature of glory, a mountebank of wit: a very human antic. He fanatically hugs his imagined greatness to him through thick and thin, as Charlie Chaplin's ragged 'little man' clings to his criterion of manners and gentility. We are fascinated to see whether Pistol can keep it up. That he can, and does, even in soliloquy, makes him a non-pareil; unique in his way, like his all-admired master. No wonder his popularity was great.

Pistol's style is always up to his own standard of excellence, because he talks mostly for himself and his imaginary enchanted audience. Humble birth, an utter lack of humour, *l'amour de l'impossible*: he shares them all with Tamburlaine. These heroes both are of imagination all compact. For Pistol is no more a player king than Tamburlaine is the wrath and vengeance of God. Pistol's absurdity is wild but entrancing, for it is only an exaggeration of every man's wish to sound well and appear bold and commanding. A satellite of Falstaff's, Pistol shares some of what Hazlitt sees as the secret of the fat knight's wit—'a masterly presence of mind, an absolute self-possession which nothing can disturb.' Pistol is never at a nonplus; never 'stalks like a peacock—a stride and a stand' or 'bites his lip with a politic regard, as who should say "There were wit in this head, an 'twould out." ' Something always comes out, magnificent if not germane. His motto is 'Mighty lines: sensible if you can; but—mighty lines!'

SHAKESPEARE AND MINE HOST OF
THE MERMAID

Souls of poets dead and gone,
What Elysium have ye known,
Happy field or mossy cavern,
Choicer than the Mermaid Tavern?

IN THE Folger Shakespeare Library in Washington is
casketed a mass of treasure. But among its many thousands of books, manuscripts, and objects which bring
Shakespeare to mind, there is one document of peculiar
and unique interest. Unique, because it is the sole personal relic of the poet in the Western Hemisphere, the
only object that we know belonged to Shakespeare, that
he held in his own hands.

At first glance this captain jewel looks prosaic enough.
A parchment indenture which records the fact that Shakespeare bought a house in Blackfriars, a couple of hundred
yards from the theatre where he trod the stage and where
so many of his plays were acted. The owner of the property was one Henry Walker, minstrel, of London. After
the scrivener had engrossed the deed of sale in duplicate,
Shakespeare signed one copy and gave it to Walker.
Walker signed the counterpart and handed it to Shakespeare, who stuffed it into his wallet. They sealed the
bargain with a cup of sack, and the bit of business was dispatched. The Folger document is the parchment that
Shakespeare took away and kept.

Plain, even bald, it seems. Shakespeare bought a house
as an investment, as thousands of lesser men have done
before and since; what more is to be said? Yet if we ex-

amine the parchment more closely we descry a brace of interesting mysteries. In the first place, *four* men are named as purchasers: 'William Shakespeare, of Stratford Vpon Avon in the countie of Warwick, gentleman, William Johnson, citizein and Vintener of London, John Jackson, and John Hemmyngs of London, gentlemen.' A subsequent clause, however, shows that the real purchaser was Shakespeare, and that the three others were trustees whom he named to act in his interest. John Hemmyngs of London, gentleman, is no other than Shakespeare's friend and fellow, the actor John Heminges who edited the Folio of 1623. But who are the two remaining friends of the poet? Nothing is known of John Jackson, gentleman, or of William Johnson, vintner. No doubt the commonness of their names has discouraged any who might attempt an identification.

Here, then, are two trusted friends of Shakespeare's who for us are no more than names. Securely they sit there in the document and scoff: 'Do you pass us by in ignorance, yet long to hear the story of his life? Much!'

This may not be borne. I will undertake you, though I break my shins in the process. Draw, if you be men as well as mysteries! Gentlemen first. . . . John Jackson, gentleman, wins his bout. With his bafflingly common name he parries every attempt, and retires smiling, his mystery still untouched.

A breathing while—then William Johnson, vintner, steps forward. At first he, too, has the best of it, with a name as utterly undistinguished as his friend's. But soft! not too fast! Vintner . . . vintner. *Q*. What conceivable connection could there be between a London vintner and Shakespeare? *A*. Well, vintners might dispense rich

Canary to thirsty actors and convivial poets. *Q.* Where? *A.* In licensed taverns. *Q.* What tavern did Shakespeare frequent? *A.* (*fortissimo*) The Mermaid! Nobody doubts that he often made one with Ben Jonson, John Donne, Christopher Brooke, and other 'right generous, jovial, and mercurial Sireniacks,' as Tom Coryate styled them, on the first Friday of every month at the famous Mermaid Tavern in Bread Street. Mind you, there is no proof of this. Never once is Shakespeare's name mentioned by any contemporary in connection with the Mermaid. Posterity has, however, taken the matter to heart. King Shakespeare not one of the bards of passion and of mirth who threw inimitable wit within the four walls of the Mermaid? A question not to be asked.

Hold, Master Johnson, enough for this once. But I have an eye of you, and will discuss the matter further when time shall serve.

Once more in the twentieth century, I am off hotfoot to see what can be made of this Mermaid notion. First, to find contemporary references to the famous tavern. Professor Sugden has collected them in his admirable *Topographical Dictionary to the Works of Shakespeare and His Fellow Dramatists*. Under 'Mermaid' I find a cluster of fascinating passages. Ben Jonson, for example, confesses in his *Epigrams*—

> That which most doth take my Muse and me
> Is a pure cup of rich Canary wine,
> Which is the Mermaid's now, but shall be mine.

So close indeed was the bond between Thirst and Thalia, Drawers and Drama, that Ben lay open to this gibe:

> That such thy drought was, and so great thy thirst,
> That all thy plays were drawn at the Mermaid first.

But what is this? 'The host in 1603 was one Johnson, as appears from the will of Alban Butler, of Clifford's Inn, who owed him 17 shillings.' A Johnson, host of the Mermaid! Could it be possible that mine host Johnson of the Mermaid and Shakespeare's friend the vintner are one and the same? The mere suggestion is exciting.

Somewhere there must be evidence to resolve this intolerable doubt. Why not a comparison of signatures? Autographs of the vintner are available. Together with Shakespeare and Jackson, he signed not only the purchase deed held by the vendor, Walker, but also, on the following day, a mortgage on the house for payment of the residue of the purchase price. The first of these documents is in the Guildhall Library, London, the other in the British Museum, and one can procure facsimiles.

Facsimiles arrive. Examining them, one notes the curious fact that on March 10, 1613, the vintner signed 'Wm Johnsonn,' but on the next day, dropping the second *n*, 'Wm Johnson'; and that Jackson followed suit with 'Jacksonn' and 'Jackson.' Yet, with these samples of his signature before me, I am still far from being able to identify Shakespeare's friend with mine host of the Mermaid. Where can one find the signature that will either clinch the identification or dissolve the theory into thin air?

When in doubt, I turn inevitably to that never-failing reservoir, the Public Record Office in Chancery Lane. Surely there must be an undiscovered record of the Mermaid Tavern preserved here. One may make a beginning with an attack on the Chancery suits indexed in the reigns of Elizabeth and James, limiting the field to those cases which deal with property in London. Before long I am rewarded by running on one which mentions the Mermaid. But what do I find? It tells me that about the turn of the seventeenth century the tavern was owned by a certain William Williamson. To discover a Williamson when I long for a Johnson is not cheering. Can the note quoted by Sugden, asserting that one Johnson was the host in 1603, be a mare's-nest?

Plus ultra is the watchword; and before relinquishing hope we can take this name, William Williamson, and launch one more drive. For variety, let us choose the index of Star Chamber: an enormous heap of Elizabethan names in the records of the court where men are had up for all sorts of lively offences, such as riots, poachings, libels, and witchcraft. Unfortunately, since this index gives no indications of place, delimitation is not easy; we may as well begin at the beginning and plod along systematically through all the names, defendants as well as plaintiffs.

The new name works like a charm. No sooner are we well into letter *A* of the index, when behold a suit brought by the Queen's Attorney-General, Coke, against a certain Sir Edmond Bainham, and, among others, William Williamson. A glance through the Attorney-General's bill —or 'information,' as it is called—finds Coke beginning the charge by declaring that on Tuesday night, March 18, 1600, the defendants did 'riotously and vnlawfully assemble themselves together at the house of one William Williamson of London, vintner, being a Comon Taverne Called the Mermayde, scituate in a street Called Bred-street.' This assembly, it appears, was the starting point for a glorious Elizabethan midnight row in the streets of London, which landed several badly battered roisterers in jail, and finally brought them penitent before the lords of the Council sitting in Star Chamber.

But can we abandon the search to plunge into this exhilarating fracas before looking about farther? The date here is 1600, and William Williamson is unquestionably host of the Mermaid. Perhaps some witnesses were examined in this case? Yes, here are depositions of several substantial friends of the tavern-keeper—two Bread Street salters, Robert Payne and Edward Prescott; a pewterer, Robert Sheppard; a constable, John Weston; and, at last, Williamson's servant, William Johnson, aged twenty-five.

This is good hunting. But the signature, on which so much depends—'*per* me William Johnsonn.' Now for a comparison. Though the first name is written out, unlike the 'W^m' of thirteen years later, the 'ohnsonn' of the last name is exactly similar, in the forming of the letters, to the signature on Shakespeare's deed, down to the break between the *o* and *h*, the doubled *n*, and the final paraph or flourish. True, the *W* of 'William' has an initial stroke which appears greatly reduced in the later signature, and the upper loop of the *J* comes to a sharp point, while that on Shakespeare's deed is rounded. Some allowance must be made for changes wrought by thirteen years, and I am persuaded that we are dealing here with the hand of one man: that William Johnson, servant in 1600 to mine host Williamson, became a member of the Vintners' Company, and stepped into Williamson's shoes as master of the Mermaid.

Yet conviction must be made absolute. Patience and a further search into the Chancery records at length yield a suit dated 1616 which gives us this: 'the Meeremayd' in Bread Street 'in the tenure of William Johnson, vintner.' That settles one point beyond cavil. To clinch the matter we must have a signature of about this date, and we turn to the vast collection of Town Depositions in Chancery. This splendid series stands our friend, and places the keystone of the arch: a deposition dated October 25, 1614, of William Johnson, of St. Mildred's, Bread Street, vintner, aged forty, and signed 'Wm Johnson.' We put the three signatures together. In the last, the 'W^m' is exactly like that on Shakespeare's deed of 1613; the 'Johnson' is the same, and the loop of the J is rounded. For the searcher, this is journey's end: Shakespeare's trusted friend is no other than mine host of the Mermaid Tavern.

The instinct of posterity is shown to be sound. The Stratford poet was more than an occasional patron of the celebrated tavern. For if Shakespeare's friend Ben Jonson felt sufficiently at home in the Mermaid to write affectionate verses about it, Shakespeare himself was so intimate with its host that he found it natural to ask him to act as his trustee in a purchase involving a large sum of money. We have added a new and fascinating figure to the circle of Shakespeare's known familiar acquaintances.

What manner of man was William Johnson, other than a vintner recognizable by his rat-coloured stockings and shining shoes? Speculation is free. Was he a genial original, like mine host of the Garter at Windsor in *The Merry Wives*, with his 'said I well, bully Hector'? That mad wag who by a trick prevented the deadly encounter between the doughty Welsh parson and the fire-eating French doctor, thus:

> Peace, I say! hear mine host of the Garter. Am I politic? Am I subtle? am I a Machiavel? Shall I lose my doctor? no; he gives me the potions and the motions. Shall I lose my parson, my priest, my Sir Hugh? no;

he gives me the proverbs and the no-verbs. Give me
thy hand, terrestrial; so;—give me thy hand, celestial;
so. Boys of art, I have deceived you both; I have directed you to wrong places: your hearts are mighty,
your skins are whole, and let burnt sack be the issue.
Come, lay their swords to pawn. Follow me, lads of
peace; follow, follow, follow.

We could wish Shakespeare no more jovial friend. But
to leave fancy, and come to the facts we can muster about
mine host Johnson, let us look at his Chancery deposition
of 1614. He pictures himself here, in professional fashion,
as down in the cellar of the rival tavern of his neighbour
Benson, the Mitre in Bread Street, tasting wines to be
taken for a debt owed to the estate of Williamson, late
master of the Mermaid. Johnson deposes 'that hee know-
eth not what quantety of the wynes . . . having the marck
of the defendant Jo: Dade upon them came to the handes,
custody, or possession of the complainant [Widow Anne
Williamson] after the death of Wm Williamson, her late
husband; for that this deponent did not take any notice
of the said defendant Dade his marck, or of any other
man's marcke, but only tasted of the wynes lately the defendant Benson's, and extended upon for debt due unto
him the said Wm Williamson by the said Benson; and such
wynes the complainant had in the Sellar of the said Benson at his howse called the Mytre in Breadstreet.'

Now that Johnson commands our keenest attention,
we find a special importance in the following record that
comes to light in the rolls of the King's Bench. An informer, one William Allen, charges that William Johnson,
of St. Mildred's in Bread Street Ward, 'a comon Vintener,' on and after [Friday] March 19, 1613, sold meat on

Fridays, being 'Fish dayes or fasting dayes.' Johnson should be fined £150,—£5 for each offence—of which the informer claims a third.

This is interesting from more than one point of view. Obviously the indictment is based on the statute of 27 Elizabeth, which ordered 'that no innholder, vintner, ale-house-keeper, common victualler, common cook, or common table-keeper shall utter or put to sale upon any Friday, Saturday, or other days appointed to be Fish Days, or any day in time of Lent, any kind of flesh vic-tuals; upon pain of forfeiture of £5; and shall suffer ten days' imprisonment without bail, mainprize, or remove, for every time so offending.'

Friday, March 19, 1613—the date of Johnson's first alleged offence—is eight days after he signed Shake-speare's mortgage. Further, it is in that period of fasting and penitence known as Lent. Moreover, the size of the fine charges him with repeating the offence on twenty-nine succeeding and additional Fridays. Finally, we recall the club of wits, 'the worshipful Fraternity of Sireniacal gen-tlemen that meet the 1st *Friday* of every month at the sign of the Mermaid in Bread Street in London.'

Law or no law, we cannot down a sense of satisfaction on learning that mine host Johnson took his chances with the enforcement agents of Meat Prohibition, and saw to it, when Will Shakespeare, Ben Jonson, Frank Beaumont, and other lads of life gathered at his Mermaid for a supper of wit and mirth, that their Parnassian palates, warmed with Canary, were not insulted with fish. They were none of your 'demure boys,' scorned by Jack Falstaff, who make so 'many fish-meals, that they fall into a kind of male greensickness.' And happily it does not appear that

Shakespeare's friend was fined and jailed for his refusal, in Mercutio's phrase, to fishify the flesh of his immortal guests. There is no record that the case ever came to trial. William Allen the informer did not get his £50. Possibly he got something less agreeable; for in those turbulent days tale-bearing must have been a risky business.

We recall that Falstaff makes a show of terrifying Hostess Quickly with a similar charge, representing it as a deadly sin as well as a crime; but she answers him stoutly:

> *Fal.* Marry, there is another indictment upon thee, for suffering flesh to be eaten in thy house, contrary to the law; for the which I think thou wilt howl [in hell].
> *Quick.* All victuallers do so: what's a joint of mutton or two in a whole Lent?

The Record Office's imposing way of making one feel that it is all-sufficient has tricked us into neglecting an inviting source of possible further information on Johnson —the records of the Worshipful Company of Vintners, preserved at Vintners' Hall, London. An application to the Clerk of the Company finds him most kind in permitting a search of the registers.

Aware that Johnson was born about 1575, we open the book at the late 1580's. Hunting carefully through the subsequent years brings us the entry we had hoped for. Under date of 11 April 1591 we read: 'for presenting of William Johnson apprenticed to William Williamson . . . xij^d.' Continuing our search, we find that our future host served a long apprenticeship—nine years—being admitted a freeman of the Company in the summer of 1600: 'for making free of William Johnson, late apprenticed to Williamson . . . xxx^d.'

Though hereby given the right to set up in trade for himself, Johnson, it seems, had to wait almost another three years before Williamson was ready to resign control of the Mermaid to him. Learning from the register that Johnson enrolled his first two apprentices in May 1603, we may conclude with some confidence that his career as master of the Mermaid dates from this year. Furthermore, we discover from another document in the Record Office that two years later, in February 1605, Johnson bound himself to pay Williamson the very large sum of £1848 within five weeks. This makes it look as though by now he had built up sufficient savings to undertake the purchase of the tavern lease. In the course of the two decades that followed, we find the names of twenty-five additional apprentices enrolled by Johnson. Clearly his undertaking was successful: there was no lack of custom and attendance at the Mermaid.

What have we learned about this newly discovered friend of Shakespeare?

Ten or eleven years younger than the poet he was. Apprenticed to Master Williamson, he spent his youth from the age of sixteen at the Mermaid, learning the mysteries of sack, Alicant, claret, muscadine, Rhenish, and charneco, making the acquaintance of the clientele, and being trained in the diplomatic and multifarious art of tavern-keeping. Though Williamson lived on till 1613, by 1603, ten years before he died, he had handed over the reins of management to the twenty-eight-year-old Johnson. Two years later we see the young man paying over to Williamson a very substantial sum, presumably the purchase price of the tavern lease. We may judge that Johnson was a credit to his training; for in his hands the

Mermaid prospered mightily, and as one of the prime taverns of London could command a distinguished and discriminating patronage. As for his character, if Shakespeare put confidence in his discretion and integrity, we can do no less.

What would we give for a chance to slip into his rat-coloured stockings and shining shoes, oversee the serving of one of his famous Friday suppers to the Mermaid club, and overhear the Olympian play of wit of which Frank Beaumont wrote to Ben Jonson:

> What things have we seen
> Done at the Mermaid! heard words that have been
> So nimble, and so full of subtill flame,
> As if that every one from whence they came
> Had meant to put his whole wit in a jest,
> And had resolv'd to live a foole, the rest
> Of his dull life. Then, when there had been thrown
> Wit able enough to justifie the Town
> For three daies past,—wit that might warrant be
> For the whole City to talk foolishly
> Till that were cancell'd—and, when that was gone,
> We left an Aire behind us, which alone
> Was able to make the two next Companies
> Right witty; though but downright fooles, more wise.

As he wrote this, Beaumont lay far from London, and dreamed of 'your full Mermaid wine'—of the sherris-sack whose operation Jack Falstaff anatomized thus:

> It ascends me into the brain; dries me there all the foolish and dull and crudy vapours which environ it; makes it apprehensive, quick, forgetive, full of nimble, fiery, and delectable shapes; which, deliver'd o'er to the voice, the tongue, which is the birth, becomes excellent wit.

For poets and wits it will do this, if rightly taken; but let a coarse earth-bound clod be drowned with sack, and he grows quarrelsome and pot-valiant. And this last, unfortunately, is what happened on a night in 1600, when a crew of roaring boys, after leaving the Mermaid—and how glad were mine host Williamson and his servant Johnson to see their backs!—raised a tumult in the sleeping streets of London. But this is another story, which demands a chapter all to itself.

'The constable is an arrant rogue, an unseasonable rogue. I have been at the cutting of a thousand better men's throats than his. And I hope to live to be at the cutting of a hundred thousand better men's throats than his within this city.'

WHAT EYE would not be arrested by a declaration so vivacious and a wish so devout? Thrashing about in the thick parchment-and-paper foliage of the Elizabethan records in Chancery Lane, intent on the hunt which ended with the discovery that Shakespeare's familiar friend, William Johnson the vintner, was no other than the host of the Mermaid Tavern, I ran upon these engaging speeches about the constable. They were part of a story of how a company of wild young sparks drank themselves quarrelsome at the Mermaid, and went whooping and hallooing through the midnight streets of London, to give bloody battle to a constable and his officers until they were overpowered.

Stories like this one make us regret that Shakespeare and his fellow playwrights lived before the day of the newspaper. Properly to measure their achievement in creating those vigorous and enthralling dramatic pictures of London life, we feel the need of hearing actual Elizabethans—the raw material of the dramatist—speak for themselves, and tell us of experience as it seemed to them. It is true that the surviving letters, memoirs, and pamphlets do much to satisfy us; yet among the manuscript records of trials in Shakespeare's London we find something more vivid than the newspaper—the depositions of witnesses. Here is a mine of living information, a mine still virtually unexplored. Here from Elizabethan lips we have racy, first-hand reports of remarkable passages of life, of accidents and crimes, all smacking of actuality; characters in search of an author; that

> pure crude fact
> Secreted from man's life when hearts beat hard,
> And brains, high-blooded, ticked [three] centuries since.

But why has this particular Star Chamber record of a very stirring brawl a stronger attraction for us than other exciting trials—for example, the story of a deer-stealing, or of a duel with rapiers in Moorfields? Well, we have already seen that the action here leads off at the Mermaid Tavern, beloved of Shakespeare and Ben Jonson. What is more, in the cloud of witnesses we shall find the testimony of Richard Kitchen, the lawyer who, as we remember, once gave bail for Christopher Marlowe, when that reckless young dramatist was in collision with the law. Further, we shall listen to William Johnson, Shakespeare's newly discovered friend. And finally, in the chief offender, Sir Edmond Bainham, we shall make the acquaintance of a notable 'angry boy,' a Captain of the Damned Crew, who here met his match in a parish constable.

Scene, the Mermaid Tavern in Bread Street, London, kept by William Williamson.

Time, Tuesday, March 18, 1600. Six o'clock in the evening.

Our first witness of what went on that night is 'poor deceased Kit Marlowe's' friend, Richard Kitchen, gentleman, aged forty-six, who says:

[While I was] walking with William Williamson in his house at 'the Mermaid' in Bread Street, Sir Edmond Bainham came into the house; upon whose coming Williamson said to me, 'Here is company coming in: and I had as list have their room as their company, for they will expect to have music here; and they shall not have any in my house.' And presently after Sir Edmond there came two or three more of the company, whereof one of them said, 'God's wounds! what shall we do in this house? for here we shall have neither music nor dicing, for the good man of this house is the precisest [*i.e.* most puritanical] man in England. We had better have gone to any tavern in London than to have come hither.' Sir Edmond and his company came to the house to supper about six of the clock in the evening, or somewhat after; and presently Williamson went from me and told me that he would go to his men and give order that there should no musicians come unto them.

Master Williamson need be no Puritan to look askance at the six wild young gentlemen with rapiers and daggers under their cloaks, who, followed by their servants, swaggered into the Mermaid, bent on wine, music, and dice. The leaders, Sir Edmond Bainham and Captain Dutton (though the tavern-keeper did not know it), were fresh from service in Ireland under the Earl of Essex, slaughtering kerns and gallowglasses. A third, Tom Badger, was not far behind them in truculence.

Williamson wanted no noise, quarrelling, or bloodshed in his house, and might take Dame Quickly's protest against Pistol out of her mouth:

If he swagger, let him not come here: no, by my faith; I must live amongst my neighbours: I'll no swaggerers: I am in good name and fame with the very best. Shut the door; there comes no swaggerers here: I have not lived all this while to have swaggering now: shut the door, I pray you.

He wished he had not let these swaggerers in; but at least he could and would shut the door against fiddlers, whose intoxicating strains would stir wine-flown spirits to unruliness; and he gave his eldest servants Johnson and Aldrich orders to that effect.

Lawyer Kitchen took his leave of the master of the tavern, and departed to his lodging. Climbing to an upper chamber of the house, the swaggering six fell to their belly-cheer, and sent the drawers skipping with calls for wine, wine, and still wine. The shades of night closed down; the moon rose over Bread Street, and the arrogant spirits of Bainham, Dutton, Badger, and their cronies rose with it. To crown their revels, they would have music; and a little before nine one of them dispatched a servant of his to fetch a 'noise'—one of the small bands of fiddlers who were usually to be found near a tavern, but 'sneaking' or lurking for fear of the constable. (Remember how Shakespeare has the First Drawer of the Boar's-Head Tavern say to the Second Drawer: 'See if thou canst find out Sneak's noise; Mistress Tearsheet would fain hear some music. Dispatch!') Let us follow this lad out on his errand, and await his return at the threshold of the house next to the tavern.

Williamson's next-door neighbour is a very old friend, a forty-seven-year-old pewterer named Robert Sheppard, who has known Williamson—apprentice and afterward householder at the Mermaid—these thirty years (ever since 1570, when Shakespeare was a small boy). As for character, he can say that 'Williamson hath, ever since he was a householder there, behaved himself very honestly and orderly in the well ordering of his house and family as any man of his trade in London, and doth not maintain any carding or dicing in his house.' Sheppard is sitting at his door in quiet converse with Robert Payne, another neighbour (who has known Williamson for a score of years), when the fiddlers, found by the roisterers' emissary, arrive, and the trouble begins.

Payne testifies:

[Sitting with Sheppard] at the next door to Williamson's house, about nine of the clock at night, I did see certain musicians come thither with a servant of one of the gentlemen, and would have come in, but could not be permitted by Williamson and his servants; whereupon the musicians, or the servant which came thither with them, made a great noise by bouncing at the door with their heels, the door being made fast against them.'

Payne and Sheppard came up to see what the row was about, and were joined by Edward Prescott, another neighbour. Prescott says, 'I reproved the serving-man for the disorder and noise, who answered me that he was sent about his master's business, and his master's business he would do.'

In the upshot, Williamson let in his three neighbours and the serving-man, but none of the fiddlers. He was much perturbed by the mounting racket abovestairs. Apprehensive potboys brought word that the loud supper party was getting dangerously out of hand, and one of the neighbours went off for the parish constable, one John Weston, a draper, who had retired for the night.

Constable Weston testifies:

I was called out of my bed about nine of the clock

at night by some of my neighbours, to go to the said Williamson's house, who told me there was some misdemeanour committed, and likely to be some mischief done. Whereupon, with as much convenient speed as I could, I did repair to the said house; and as I came near unto the door, I did see divers persons standing there, who upon sight of me said, 'Yonder comes the constable!' and withal ran away from the door; they being musicians, as near as I could judge by the moonlight, for I perceived them to have something under their cloaks. And then I knocked at the door and was let in, and went presently [upstairs] into the room where Badger and the rest of the gentlemen were. (I do know Thomas Badger, and have known him for the space of these two years or thereabouts, but do not know any of the other gentlemen.)

And upon my coming, Badger took notice of me, and complained himself to me of Williamson, that he would not suffer them to have music there. Whereupon I charged them to keep her majesty's peace, and to behave themselves like gentlemen. And thereupon one of the gentlemen, which was said to be Sir Edmond Bainham, did desire to speak with Williamson; and presently therewithal came down into a room where Williamson was with Robert Payne, Edward Prescott, and Robert Sheppard, and there spake to Payne (thinking he had been Williamson), and told him that he was sorry that the constable was sent for; and that he thought he might have obtained so much favour as to [have] had some music there. Whereunto Williamson answered, that he did not use to permit any music in his house at that time of night. And then Sir Edmond replied and said, that if they might have so much favour as to stay there some small time, they would depart in quiet manner, without further trouble of any;—using other discreet speeches which I do not now certainly remember.

And further, Williamson willed me to persuade them to go quietly out of the house, for that he was afraid they would do some hurt to him or his wife or servants; and said further to me, that he would willingly give them their reckoning to be quietly rid of them.

Neighbour Sheppard remembers Sir Edmond's expressions as somewhat more offensive:

Taking Payne to be the master of the house, [Sir Edmond] said unto him that he knew her majesty's laws and what belonged to government better than he did, and so he thought the rest of his company did likewise; and therefore thought himself very hardly dealt with to have a constable sent unto them.

Obviously it was past closing time, and the tipplers knew it. But they also knew that, however much Williamson wished them gone, it would be a ticklish thing, numerous and reckless as they were, for him to try to eject them. Constable Weston, having delivered his warning and received assurances of good behaviour, went home to his interrupted rest.

The gallants were by now more than three parts fuddled and cup-shot. To their first grievance, the prohibition of fiddlers, had been added this second, the sending up of the constable to admonish them. The more they drank and dizzily reflected on their wrong, the more it rankled. They fell to easing 'their stomachs with their bitter tongues'; and when, as the night wore on, Williamson went up to reason with them, they gave him saucy and outrageous language. Constabulary interference had been the last straw; and they began to study malicious knavery—especially the annihilation of constables.

Williamson, no longer a young man, was more than

tired of his heady guests. It was far past his bedtime; and about ten o'clock he called his eldest servants, William Johnson—Shakespeare's friend, who in three years was to step in as master of the Mermaid—and Edward Aldrich, to him for their final instructions. Examined in court on the question whether the brawling began in the Mermaid, Johnson testifies:

> Sir Edmond Bainham and his company did depart from the house of my master about eleven of the clock at night in peaceable manner. Williamson was in his chamber at such time as Sir Edmond Bainham and his company departed thence. Williamson, before he went up into his chamber, willed me and my fellow-servants to stay by them [the company], but not to reply or give any words of offence unto them, whatsoever they should say, but to bear any words which they should say as he himself had done. Neither Sir Edmond Bainham nor any other in his company did throw off their upper garments, nor did draw any manner of weapon, to my knowledge, at the time of their departure from the house.

Young Aldrich corroborates his fellow-servant Johnson as to the time of the roisterers' departure, and gives his version of Williamson's words as follows:

> 'You know what hard words they have given me, and I do bear it; and therefore I would that by all means you do bear anything that they shall say.' And further, Sir Edmond and his company did quietly depart out of the house without casting off any of their upper garments, or drawing of any weapons, whilst they were in my sight; and so I left them, and locked up the doors after them. But Sir Edmond Bainham, before he went out of the house, did give his cloak to his man and willed him to hie him home and make a fire in his chamber, and he would come presently.

The swashbucklers were out of the house without violence or blows struck. With what relief did Johnson and
Aldrich shoot the bolts home behind the last well-dressed
and drunken guest! The fellow-servants exchanged a look,
and went up to a welcome bed. Their conjecture of the
time as 'about eleven' when the riotous pot-companions
tumbled out of the tavern is conservative, doubtless made
so to soften the censure which might fall on the Mermaid
for keeping late hours; for when the watch two streets
away towards St. Paul's first heard uproar in the
street, it was, according to their calculation, 'about
midnight.'

The soft air of an early spring night recalled the winish
spirits to their purpose of punishing the officers of the
watch, whose duty it was to stop and question all who
walked the streets of London at this late hour. When they
threw their cloaks to their servants, that rapier arms might
have free play, our six roaring boys were far from the
cautious mood in which Valentine (in Beaumont and
Fletcher's *Wit without Money*) asks: 'Draw me a map
from the Mermaid; I mean a midnight map to 'scape the
watches.' On the contrary, they were bent on striking
terror to the hearts of all watchmen and constables who
might cross their path. The more the better. And what
their army lacked in numbers they made up in noise.
'Full of supper and distempering draughts,' and reeling-
ripe for mischief, they made a formidable show with their
blades flashing in the moonlight. The two men and a boy
of the Friday Street watch who first sighted this warlike front rolling down upon them might be pardoned if
they were tempted to follow Dogberry's advice in *Much
Ado*:

Master Constable Dogberry. This is your charge: you shall comprehend all vagrom men; you are to bid any man stand, in the prince's name.

Watch. How if 'a will not stand?

Dogb. Why then, take no note of him, but let him go; and presently call the rest of the watch together, and thank God you are rid of a knave.

Verges. If he will not stand when he is bidden, he is none of the prince's subjects. . . .

Dogb. Well, you are to . . . bid those that are drunk get them to bed.

Watch. How if they will not?

Dogb. Why then, let them alone till they are sober.

The Friday Street constable was named, not Dogberry, but Doughty; and at the corner of Friday and Watling Streets he had posted James Muggins, a haberdasher aged forty-seven, Thomas Bastwicke, a sixty-year-old salter, and an apprentice. These men, outnumbered as they were, and armed only with halberds—a blade and spearhead mounted on a long staff—made a commendable but futile attempt to quiet the Sons of Belial, disguised as gentlemen, who descended on them.

Let Muggins tell his story:

About 12 of the clock at night, I and Thomas Bastwicke and one other (three watchmen under one Doughty, a constable in Friday Street), being placed at the corner of Friday Street, heard a noise of whooping and hallooing by divers persons whose names I know not; and seeing them coming with their swords drawn, without cloaks, I and the other two watchmen in my company went unto them; and then, putting off my hat, I did desire them to make less noise and to be quiet. And one of them (whose name I know not) then asked of me what I was. And I answered, 'One of the Queen's watch.' And he replied, 'Then art a rogue,'

and withal laid his hand upon my halberd, endeavouring
to take it from me, and struck me on the head with his
sword, and on the face with his hand. And one other of
the company (whose name I know not) was ready with
his sword to have run me through, and so had done,
but that one of their company took him and turned
him about.

Bastwicke, the old watchman, corroborates Muggins's
account in detail, and adds:

> I came to one of the company, whose name I know
> not [obviously Sir Edmond Bainham], with my hat in
> my hand, and said unto him, 'Good gentleman, be
> quiet.' 'God's wounds!' said he, and took me by the
> beard, saying, 'Dost thou make but a gentleman of me?
> I am a knight!' and withal shook me by the beard in
> such sort as he made my eyes water abundantly. And
> another of the disordered company, whose name I
> know not, did thrust at me with a sword or rapier, and
> he was called away by another of his company who said
> I should not be hurt because I was an old man; and so
> they departed.

For the 'terrible boys' this was no victory at all; they
wanted watchmen worthy of their steel. The band turned
west down Watling Street, and made for St. Augustine's
Gate into Paul's Churchyard. To reach the Strand, where
Bainham, Dutton, and Badger had their lodgings, they
must pass St. Gregory's by St. Paul's, then down Bowyers' Row and out through London Wall at Ludgate.
Stubborn opposition, however, awaited them in Paul's
Churchyard. In that enclosure there was something more
than the dark and shuttered fronts of booksellers' shops
such as the Angel, kept by Andrew Wise, which had for
present sale copies of *The History of Henrie the Fourth*

... *With the humorous conceits of Sir Iohn Falstaffe*, by William Shakespeare, a playwright who at that moment was doubtless sleeping quietly in his bed across the river in Southwark.

James Briggs, a forty-three-year-old blacksmith, constable of St. Gregory's, was keeping watch in St. Paul's Churchyard, with seven or more men under him. Catching the glint of drawn swords approaching from the east through St. Augustine's Gate, Briggs told off four of his halberdiers to go and look into it.

One of these was Thomas Rice, a clothworker aged twenty-five; and he tells a lively tale as follows:

At midnight, James Briggs, constable in St. Gregory's parish, together with me and others of the watch, were standing at Pullford's door near unto Paul's Chain; at which time we saw a company coming from Watling Street end in their doublets and hose, with their swords drawn in their hands. And thereupon James Briggs the constable sent me, Edward Smith, Hugh Williams, and one other of the watch named Jarvys, unto the said persons to inquire what the matter was. And when I and those in my company came near them, I demanded of them what they were, and what the reason was why they were with their swords drawn. Whereupon Badger, one of the company, came forth from the rest, and sware, 'God's wounds! what do you here with your halberds? If you will not stand away, I will run you through.'

And thereupon the said Badger and his company [came] all together with their swords drawn; and I and the rest of my company kept them back with our halberds, until at last Hugh Williams, lifting up his halberd to strike at them, they brake in with their swords, and had the said Williams down. And Sir Edmond

Bainham did then cut Williams in the head, and Captain Dutton with his sword or rapier ran him through the jerkin, doublet, and shirt on his right side, and yet missed his body. And Sir Edmond Bainham having gotten Williams his halberd from him, Sir Edmond and his company passed me and those which were then in my company. Whereupon Constable Briggs with the rest of his company came to rescue us. And then Sir Edmond with his halberd knocked down the said constable; and went on from thence and did hurt one Abraham Parnell, one other of the watchmen, in the wrist.

One of these watchmen, an apprentice named Richard Exoll, adds:

I was knocked down with a halberd twice at the least, and was sore hurt; and I think in my conscience that Briggs had been slain if he had not been well defended by me and other watchmen.

Bainham worked sanguinary havoc among the watch with their own weapon; but Briggs and Williams, though wounded and momentarily down, were far from out—as the rioters were soon to discover.

After hearing the watch's view of the battle, it is interesting to read the drunken gentlemen's very innocent-and-injured account of it, prepared for their defence in court:

These defendants did take the ordinary ways towards their lodgings, in which way they happened, at or about the gate which is at or near the west end of Watling Street, to come amongst certain watchmen (as since these defendants understand them to be, but at that time these defendants—it being in the night—did not on the sudden discern what they were, *viz.*, either watchmen or others) who, without making themselves

known to be the watch, or requiring these defendants
(to their hearing) to stay, did bend their weapons towards these defendants as though they had a purpose to
have made an assault; whereupon these defendants did
draw their weapons, and afterwards some strokes
passed between them, wherein these defendants (or
most of them) received divers blows and wounds, to
the great effusion of the blood of some of them, and
some of them were stricken down divers times to the
ground, so as they were all greatly astonied and
amazed; which affray was committed in or on two
several places in the high street, but not within the
churchyard of St. Paul's (to these defendants' knowledge). But therein what hurt was done to others, [or]
by whom and in what manner the same was done, these
defendants do not know, for that the same was a sudden uproar and fury raised to the great affright and
astonishment of these defendants. But if in the said
affray any hurt hath been done, or offence committed
by these defendants or by their means, they are heartily
sorry and grieved for the same, and do in all humble-
ness submit themselves to the grave, honourable, and
favourable censure of this most honourable Court.

Very innocent, surprised, and apologetic. But we
have yet to hear the outcome of the fray as the watch
saw it.

Dutton and Bainham were in a drunken fury, and
struck to kill. In this crisis, as Watchman Exoll tells us,
'the watch, for safeguard of their lives, were enforced to
cry out for help; and upon that cry the said disordered
persons fled towards Ludgate. And I, with the constable
and the rest of the watch, followed towards Ludgate,
and there and near thereabouts divers of them were
taken.'

The watch, although they called for help, evened up

scores with Bainham and Dutton, whom they left down near Ludgate, badly damaged and unable to move, while they chased and captured Tom Badger and one William Grantham. The rest made good their escape. Several citizens—a constable and some haberdashers in and about Bowyers' Row and Ludgate, where the running fight took place—rolled out of bed at the shouts for aid, and dashed into the dark street to lend a hand. We can piece together the details from their testimony.

Nicholas Dethicke, a haberdasher:

> I did hear a very great outcry and uproar in the streets, and heard people cry 'Murder! Murder!' Whereupon I presently arose and went forth into a place called Bowyers' Row near Ludgate; and then and there perceived that there had been a great affray and outrage done by Sir Edmond Bainham, Captain Dutton, and others. And perceiving the said Sir Edmond to be hurt in the same affray and outrage, I took him by the arm and went with him to a barber's shop thereby, where he was dressed.

Bainham was supported on the other side by another haberdasher, Henry Colthurste, who corroborates this story.

Dethicke says he found Bainham and Dutton 'sore hurt and wounded'; and 'what with their hurts and what with the distemperature of drink, [they] did exceedingly stagger in their going as they passed along, and were fain to be holden up. And in the time they were dressed of their hurts, did show great tokens of their insobriety, not fit to be spoken of in this honourable Court.'

Thomas Langwith, a haberdasher who helped to get Dutton back up the street to the barber's shop in the Churchyard by Paul's Chain, deposes:

I found Captain Dutton sitting upon the bench near Ludgate, being hurt, and heard [him] desire to go to a surgeon's to be dressed. And so he rose and went; and upon the way in Ludgate Street, Dutton said, 'If I live, I will be revenged of this city. I will set fire on it.'

Dethicke relates further that 'as he [Sir Edmond] was in dressing, Captain Dutton, being overcome with drink, came into the barber's shop: unto whom Sir Edmond (also overcome with drink) then said, "How dost thou, Tom? I doubt not but we shall have a day [*i.e.* of revenge] shortly for this. And I hope to be at the sacking of this city." And immediately upon the uttering of these speeches, the said Dutton fell asleep. And afterwards, upon the multiplying of speeches, Sir Edmond swore by God's wounds that if he had but fifty horse, he could overcome the city.'

Constable Briggs and more of his men joined the gathering in the barber's shop, bringing in Tom Badger and the fourth prisoner, William Grantham. Briggs and his watch had wounds of their own to be looked to. Says Exoll, of the watch:

Sir Edmond Bainham, seeing Briggs the constable come into the barber's shop, said, 'God's wounds! art thou alive yet? I had thought thou hadst been slain, or else I would have run my rapier up to the hilts in thee, for I have been sundry times troubled with watches.'

Rice, of the watch, recalls a fiery threat: 'Sir Edmond said, "If I live, I will be revenged of thee, Briggs, if thy name be Briggs. I will fire thee and this city."'

Thomas Smith, another haberdasher, remembers something very insulting: '[Sir Edmond] willed Briggs the constable to keep on his hat to keep in his cuckold's horns.'

When the barber had finished binding up the assorted wounds, and Tom Dutton had been shaken out of his stupor, the signal was given. Briggs and his watch marched the four bandaged revellers back through Paul's Churchyard, up Old Change to Cheapside, and so eastward to the Compter in Wood Street—the jail a few yards north of the Mermaid Tavern where, a few hours before, this memorable night had begun. Bainham's and Dutton's tongues had not been arrested, and the grim watch had to listen to more abuse and threats as they trudged along.

Rice, of the watch:

Captain Dutton, as he was passing from the barber's shop towards the Compter, said, 'What do these halberds here? There need not so many halberds with me, now I am hurt.' 'Nay,' said one of the company, 'the halberds go not with you, they go with the constable.' 'The constable,' said Dutton, 'is an arrant rogue, an unseasonable rogue. I have been at the cutting of a thousand better men's throats than his. And I hope to live to be at the cutting of a hundred thousand better men's throats than his within this city.'

Exoll, of the watch:

Captain Dutton, as he went towards the Compter, said that the constables and watchmen were a company of rogues, rascals, villains . . . and unseasonable slaves. And that if ever any of them chanced to come under his command, he would plague the rogues for that night's work.

Weylde, the Ludgate constable, who, like the haberdashers, had left his bed at the cries of 'Murder!':

Captain Dutton, as he was . . . going along the Old Change, swore these horrible oaths, *viz.*, 'By the blood and wounds of God, I hope ere it be long to see the throats of ten thousand of you cut.'

When he saw the gate of the jail waiting for him, Sir Edmond hurled his final defiance at Constable Briggs. This was Tuesday night; and Sir Edmond had intended to leave London within three days—before Easter Sunday. Now, however, he had earned the privilege of spending that holy tide in jail.

Briggs the constable relates that 'when Sir Edmond Bainham came to the Compter gate, he said to me, "Sirrah, is thy name Briggs? and dost thou mean to have me into this place (meaning the Compter)? I will make thee repent it, for I meant to have gone out of town within these three days, but now I will not go these three weeks. For what with making of friends, and what with giving of bribes, I will be revenged of thee, and be thy undoing." '

Exoll, of the watch:

> Sir Edmond at the Compter gate also said that he thought to have gone out of town within three or four days; but now he would stay a quarter of a year. . . . And that he would have the constable in the Compter within ten days, and would not leave him whilst he was worth a groat.

It seems pretty clear that Bainham's and Dutton's alcoholic abuse and threats of revenge voice the Elizabethan antagonism, bred of the rise of the industrial and mercantile classes, between courtier and citizen, gentleman and tradesman, heir and self-made man. Every thrust of the rapier on the night of our story was a drunken assertion of privilege; every hearty counterblow of the halberd was a knock-down argument for a common law over every Englishman. The watch, under the frothy insults— that they were base rascals, to be cuckolded by their betters—contented themselves with a glance at the bandaged gentlemen headed for jail, and with the cool retort, 'Nay, the halberds go not with you, they go with the constable.'

The pertinacious parish constable, Blacksmith Briggs, commands our admiration. He saw these murderous gentlemen behind the bars, and would risk what they and their possible friends in high places might do to him afterwards.

Briggs the constable laid down his halberd three centuries ago; yet do we not meet him whenever we walk abroad in the streets of London to-day? He has changed his doublet and hose for a suit of uniform blue, but under it he is unmistakably the same Briggs, embodiment of English order. A Londoner can take Carlyle's famous sentence about Shakespeare, transpose the names 'Shakespeare' and 'Parish-Constable,' and yet do truth no violence:

> Wheresoever, under what sort of Shakespeare soever, English men and women are, they will say to one another, 'Yes, this Parish-Constable is ours; we produced him, we speak and think by him; we are of one blood and kind with him.'

It is satisfying to learn that our roaring boys spent several cooling weeks in prison. Their case did not come up before the lords in Star Chamber until June 6, more than two months and a half after their midnight battle. John Hawarde's notes of the trial are preserved in his *Reportes del Cases in Camera Stellata*. After rehearsing the charge, the confession and submission of the culprits, and their statement that all was done 'in drink and heat,' Hawarde reports that each of the gentlemen was fined £200 and his jail fees. This sentence the Court declared was 'gracious and favourable.'

Williamson of the Mermaid was at length acquitted after some debate; for at first the Chief Justice, the Lord Treasurer, and the Lord Keeper 'would have fined him £40 because he was a *Causa sine qua non*. But because he was known to be an honest man, and of good government, and would not suffer music or illegal games in his house, and sent for the constable for to keep good order, he was acquitted by the sentence. And it was there delivered that no taverner or alekeeper ought to suffer or receive company after 9 o'clock; and because drunkenness is now so common and general and odious (as to drink "by bushel measure," "dozen," and "yards"), it was delivered as law that a common drunkard may be bound for his good behaviour.'

Philip Gawdy's report in a letter to his brother is briefer:

> Sir Edward Baynam, Tom Dutton, Tom Badger and some others, being somewhat merry, set one night upon the watch; they were brought in upon a riot into the Star Chamber, he fined at 500 marks, the rest at £200 apiece, and their oversight much noted.

If we were to pursue the tale of Bainham, that captain of the Damned Crew whom William Camden calls 'a most lascivious man, and a contemner of magistrates,' we should find him in the forefront of Essex's rebellion, condemned to death, and at length heavily fined and pardoned; two years later, in 1603, when Elizabeth lay dying, some 'dangerous companions were clapt up,' among them Bainham, who for some 'desperate speeches' against James was briefly committed to the Marshalsea. In the subsequent Gunpowder Plot he turns up again as the conspirators' messenger to the Pope:

> Sir Edmond Baynam, Prince of the Damned Crew
> Unto the Pope was sent with tidings new
> Him to acquaint with this damned Powder Treason.

But we shall keep to our theme, which is Constable *versus* Drunken Rowdy, by closing with some verses written in the summer after the trial in Star Chamber. In lively fashion they dramatize Captain Sir Edmond Bainham and Tom Dutton in their notorious post-Mermaid riot:

> Hang him, base gull! I'll stab him, by the Lord!
> If he presume to speak but half a word,
> I'll paunch the villain with my rapier's point,
> Or hew him with my falchion joint by joint.
> Through both his cheeks my poniard he shall have,
> Or mincepie-like I'll mangle out the slave.
> Ask who I am, you whoreson frieze-gown patch?
> Call me before the constable or watch?
> Cannot a captain walk the Queen's highway?
> 'Swounds! Who d'ye speak to? Know ye, villains, ha?
> You drunken peasants, runs your tongues on wheels?
> Long you to see your guts about your heels?
> Dost love me, Tom? Let go my rapier then!
> Persuade me not from killing nine or ten.
> I care no more to kill them in bravado
> Than for to drink a pipe of *Trinidado*.[1]
> My mind to patience never will restore me
> Until their blood do gush in streams before me.
> Thus doth *Sir Launcelot* in his drunken stagger
> Swear, curse, and rail, threaten, protest, and swagger.
> But being next day to sober answer brought,
> He's not the man can breed so base a thought.

This telling and topical thrust is from *The Letting of Humours Blood in the Head-Vein* (1600); and the author is Samuel Rowlands, merchant. What makes the satire

---

[1] That is, than to smoke a pipe of tobacco.

piquant is to observe that for this same year Rowlands
served as constable of East Smithfield. We recall that it
was Constable James Briggs, a blacksmith, who arrested
Bainham. Here we find his colleague in preserving the
Queen's peace, Samuel Rowlands, rubbing in and under-
lining their victory over the sons of Belial.

Time brings his revolutions. Not long ago it would
have seemed preposterous to look for a cutting verse-
satire from a London bobby. But now that the Metro-
politan Police recruits from the Universities, we may confidently expect something pretty and apt on the vapour-
ings of a West End bounder gone lion-drunk.

SHAKESPEARE MOURNS A GODLY BREWER

How shall one explain the complex satisfaction given by a jig-saw puzzle, one of the sawed-up-picture variety? The jumbled pieces have little interest taken separately, until two or more can be made to fit together. Then, and suddenly, not only do they acquire meaning, a relation to each other, but from them a super-meaning, a kind of third dimension—the picture—begins to grow.

Of recent years some contributions to our knowledge of Shakespeare have come to life in the same fruitful way. For example, here are two long-known and apparently isolated fragments: first, a set of verses in warm and familiar praise of Shakespeare's achievement in drama, contributed to the First Folio by an Oxford scholar and translator, Leonard Digges; and second, there is the naming by Shakespeare in his will of a certain Thomas Russell, esquire, to supervise its execution. What possible connection could there be between two such items, to all appearances so remote from each other? Then I find proof not only that Shakespeare's chosen friend Thomas Russell had been Leonard Digges's stepfather since Leonard was twelve years old, but also that the Russell–Digges family lived close by Stratford-on-Avon at least from 1600 to 1611 or 1612. As a result of this fitting-together, the picture—Shakespeare's life—gains somewhat in relief and distinctness. Moreover, we have here produced (if it were needed) a new documentary proof of the identity of the gentleman of Stratford with the dramatist of London.

This sort of thing warns us that the happy phenomenon may occur again at any moment. Old, neglected items in the biographical gallimaufry may marry, produce something new, and be themselves rejuvenated in the process. To set the stage for another such occurrence, the essential is to bear in mind all the names of persons and places in any way connected with Shakespeare, and then to stand by to catch any clue that offers.

One such disregarded name is that of the 'John Jackson of London, gentleman,' who, together with Shakespeare's partner John Heminges the actor and mine host William Johnson of the Mermaid, took part with the poet in his purchase of the Blackfriars Gate-House in 1613.

John Jackson. Not at all promising. Almost as common and indistinguishable a name as William Johnson. Still, we have certain points to aid us. Shakespeare's John Jackson has the rank of gentleman, and he lives in London. Moreover, there are examples of his signature on Shakespeare's Conveyance and Mortgage. And we note that in subscribing his strongly individualized signature he exuberantly repeats the 'n' in 'Jacksonn' and makes his capital J's with redoubled loops like true-love knots. In identification, these peculiarities should prove useful.

Roving through the voluminous files of the Court of King's Bench at the Record Office, our eye is caught by a name among the London actions brought in 1617, the year after Shakespeare's death. Here is a 'John Jackson, gentleman, and Jane his wife, executrix of Jacob James, executor of Elias James of London, brewer,' suing for a debt contracted in the spring of 1610 [K.B.27/1460/589]. Is this our John Jackson, gentleman, Shakespeare's trustee, or some other? Apparently there is no means of telling, since the court record naturally carries no signatures.

But is there not another possible Shakespeare clue here? 'Elias James' faintly rings a far-off bell. Where have we heard that unusual collocation of names before? Yes, among 'Verses ascribed to Shakespeare' there is an epitaph on Elias James. It was found among the Rawlinson Manuscripts in the Bodleian Library (Rawl. Poet. MS. 160, f.41) and is associated there with verses of about 1630 to 1640. Spelling modernized, it runs as follows:

An Epitaph

When God was pleas'd (the world unwilling yet),
Elias James to Nature paid his debt,
And here reposeth. As he liv'd he died,
The saying in him strongly verified,
Such life, such death. Then, the known truth to tell,
He liv'd a godly life, and died as well.

Wm. Shakespeare.

Of the biographers who reprint this epitaph, Sir Edmund Chambers vouchsafes no comment on it, while the late Dr. J. Q. Adams ventures an unsupported guess that James lived near Stratford-on-Avon.

Are we any better off than we were before? The devil's advocate reminds us that all we have so far is a circular chain of possibilities. Shakespeare *may* have written this epitaph on Elias James, who *may* be the Elias James mentioned in our 1617 suit, whose executor Jacob James's widow Jane married John Jackson, gentleman, who *may* be Shakespeare's trustee. Yet, since we have gone so far a-maying, let us see if somehow the 'may' can be turned into something stronger.

Talk of executors and wills sends us off hotfoot to Somerset House, in quest of the testament of Elias James, brewer. And we find the registered copy of it without any trouble (P.C.C. 83 Wingfield):

> The Sixteenth daye of September Anno Domini 1610. In the name of God Amen I Elias James of the Citie of London in the parishe of Sainct Andrew in the Warde of Castle Baynard Brewer sicke in Bodye ... I bequeathe ... my bodye to be buryed in the parishe churche of Sainct Andrew, &c.

And the will was proved 26 September 1610 by ... Jacob James brother of the testator.

These few lines at once give us three very encouraging facts: (*a*) Elias James the brewer died in September 1610, when Shakespeare, approaching the end of his residence in London, was still quite capable of producing a verse epitaph; (*b*) Elias James was to be buried in his parish church, St. Andrew by the Wardrobe. This stood diagonally across the street from the Blackfriars Gate-House in Puddle Dock Hill which Shakespeare purchased two and a half years later; (*c*) Elias James's executor is his brother Jacob, which tallies with the description in the King's Bench suit named above.

Next we search out the registered will of Jacob James, gentleman (P.C.C. 76 Capell), and find that it was made in January 1613 and proved in August of the same year by his widow Jane.   Though domiciled a few streets to the eastward in the parish of St. Michael Queenhithe, Vintry Ward, Jacob likewise directs his body to be buried in the church of St. Andrew by the Wardrobe. An interesting item in his will is his token bequest of five pounds to 'John Jackson.' Evidently we are dealing with the same persons who figured in the King's Bench suit: and the John Jackson whom Jacob's widow Jane married was her husband's friend.

On taking stock, we find we are clearly better off than we were. We have brought Elias James out of nowhere into close neighbourhood of time and place with William Shakespeare. And it remains possible that Shakespeare's friend John Jackson is identical with the John Jackson who married Elias James's sister-in-law Jane.

While we are amongst the wills, why not try for John Jackson's? Almost at once we turn up the copy of what must be the will of the gentleman connected with the James family (38 Clarke): date, 26 January 1624/5; John Jackson, of St. Thomas the Apostle in Vintry Ward, gentleman; for he has a wife Jane, who took probate of his will on 12 April 1625, and like Elias and Jacob James, he wishes his body to be buried in the church of St. Andrew by the Wardrobe, adjoining Blackfriars. Unluckily the original will, by whose signature we could at once test the identification we have surmised, is not forthcoming.

Yet there may be other means of arriving at the conclusion, for a prominent item in his will mentions 'all his houses and lands in Kingston-upon-Hull.' With this in mind we return to the Record Office. And when we obtain, from a Chancery proceeding of 1601/2, concerning land in Kingston-upon-Hull (*Dalton v. Lyster*, C24/290) the deposition of 'John Jackson of London, gentleman, aged 26,' with a signature which tallies, true-love 'J's, doubled 'n,' terminal paraph and all, with that of Shakespeare's friend on the poet's conveyance of the Blackfriars Gate-House, we may conclude that the chase is closing in. And on getting two more depositions with the same signature, one (*Hanbury v. Harrys*, C24/426) of 1615/6 of John Jackson of the parish of St. Michael Queenhithe, London, gentleman, aged forty, and the other (*Cotes v. Cotes*, C24/449) of 1618 of the same, esquire, aged forty-four, we may feel we have all the reasonable proof we need. Another step forward is the finding of an abstract of pedigree of the James family (Bodl. MS. Rawl. B429, f. 35ᵛ), in which Elias James is said to have died unmarried.

We have thus connected Shakespeare's friend and trustee John Jackson with the family of Elias James, brewer, who in 1610 died a bachelor and was buried in his church adjoining the Precinct of the Blackfriars where Shakespeare's company played, and diagonally across the street from the house he later purchased. Though there is no proof as yet that the Elias James of the epitaph and Elias James the brewer of St. Andrew by the Wardrobe are one and the same, the unusualness of the name makes the identification highly probable. No one has found any other Elias James.

Now let us look once more at the epitaph, this time at its language. These lines, while not distinguished, are competent memorial verse. The phrasing is simple, strong, and memorable. An inspection of the turns of thought and choice of words shows that many of them are not un-Shakespearean. Following are passages from the epitaph and extracts from the plays and poems to compare with them.

> *When God was pleas'd* (*the world unwilling yet*)
> Peace to his soul, if God's good pleasure be
> (*2 Henry VI* 3.3.26.)

If the heavens had been pleased, would we had so
    ended!   (*Tw. Night* 2.1.21.)

The world will wail thee [a bachelor] like a makeless
    wife.   (*Sonn.* 9.4.)

Elias James to Nature paid his debt

Nature craves All dues be render'd to their owners
              (*Troil. & Cress.* 2.2.173.)

For it [heaven] requires the royal debt it lent you
              (*Rich. III* 2.2.95.)

He that dies pays all debts
              (*Temp.* 3.2.140.)

And here reposeth. As he liv'd he died,

Remembering that Elias James of St. Andrew's died unmarried, it is interesting to compare the words 'as he
liv'd he died' with a favourite phrase of Shakespeare's
about confirmed celibacy:

Grows, lives and dies in single blessedness.
So will I grow, so live, so die, my lord.
            (*Mid. N.D.* 1.1.78–79.)

Marry that will, I live and die a maid
            (*All's Well* 4.2.74.)

Though to itself it only live and die.
            (*Sonn.* 94.10.)

The saying in him strongly verified,
'Such life, such death.'
The saying did not hold In him
            (*Rich. III* 2.4.16.)

Unless the adage must be verified
That 'beggars mounted run their horse to death'
            (*3 Henry VI* 1.4.126.)

So bad a death argues a monstrous life.

(2 Henry VI 3.3.31.)

Then the known truth to tell,
He liv'd a godly life, and died as well.

And uses a known truth to pass a thousand nothings with.

(All's Well 2.5.32.)

So much for the epitaph. Though naturally it gives no hint of James's view of Shakespeare's dramatic poetry, we may allow him taste enough to have been fond of it. For we recall the ominous couplet:

> *No epitaph adorn his baser hearse*
> *That in his lifetime cares not for a verse!*

Now for a glance at the origin and connections of Elias James, who lived from about 1578 to 1610. He came of a Dutch family: his grandfather Jacob van Hawstert was an immigrant. Dropping the surname, Jacob's children adopted the English form of his baptismal name, James. They were all probably members of the Dutch congregation in London. The eldest son, Roger James, prospered as a beer-brewer. Living at the Ram's Head brewery in All Saints Barking, he leased two other great breweries on the other side of the Tower of London—the Hart's Horn and the Hermitage or Swan's Nest. (The latter, whose name is preserved today in the Hermitage Entrance and Hermitage Basin of the London Docks, was the inheritance of John Stepkin, gentleman, son-in-law and victim of Justice William Gardiner, the enemy of Francis Langley and Shakespeare.) Roger James (P.C.C. 20 Harrington) left a large family of children, all sons but one, of whom the eldest, Roger junior (Elias's first cousin), grew so wealthy as to be pricked Sheriff of London in 1605, and was later knighted. No doubt he is the merchant James said to have been a partisan of the Earl of Essex, 1601: 'James and Jackson, rich merchants, were of this faction.' (S.P. 12/278/64.)

Elias's father was Jacob van Hawstert's third son Dericke (Theodore) James, also a beer-brewer. Dericke leased and lived at the great brewery between Puddle Wharf and Baynard's Castle, at the foot of Puddle Dock Hill. At his death on New Year's Day, 1590, the inventory of the lease and stock of the brewery amounted to £806 10s. 3d. (P.C.C. 1 Drury; *Lib. Test. Exam. Cur. Cons. Lond.* 1609–11, p. 365.) By his wife Marie, a widow with two daughters when she married him, Dericke had three sons: Abraham, Elias, and Jacob, and several daughters, one of whom married a knight. Abraham died in 1600, Marie the mother in 1603 (P.C.C. 86 Bolein). After this, Elias carried on the business of the brewery. Dying unmarried in September 1610, he left it to his 'loving brother' Jacob. The latter survived him less than three years. The great wealth of the family is indicated by Jacob's legacies of £1000 each to his three daughters. His widow Jane soon married his friend and neighbour John Jackson, and is said to have brought him most of Jacob's £8000 estate.

If the brewery at Puddle Wharf where the Jameses lived was valued, lease and stock, in 1590 at over eight hundred pounds, it was no small affair. John Stow, indeed, in his perambulation of Castle Baynard Ward, notices it. Proceeding westward along Thames Street, Stow mentions Paul's Wharf, Scrupes Inn, Burley House, Baynard's Castle, divers wood-wharves, and then 'there is a great Brewhouse, and Puddle wharfe, a water gate into the Thames . . .' Like the Hermitage beyond the Tower, the James brewhouse at Puddle Wharf banked on the river, as one of the 'twenty great Brewhouses or more, situate on the Thames side, from Milford-Stairs in Fleet-street, till below St. Katharine's.'

Stow remarks, 'the Brewers for the more part remain near to the friendly water of Thames.' Friendly not only because it bore the shipping to Queenhithe and Billings-gate with sea-coal for their furnaces, and stores of hops and hard, straw-dried yellow malt, but also because they used Thames water for their 'liquor.' For in spite of Nashe's observation that brewers grow rich 'by retayling filthy Thames water,' that same water was generally held to produce the best beer (Harrison, *Descr. of England*, New Shak. Soc., I. 160). More than that, English beer, with London beer made of filthy Thames water at the head, was so celebrated and sought after that despite the diligent bezzling and beer-bathing of English tosspots, bench-whistlers, and lick-wimbles, 'like dromedaries in the caravana, drinking for the thirst past, for the thirst present, and for the thirst to come,' the hard-working brewers of England made enough not only to satisfy the home mar-ket, but to supply a large export trade as well. Among the French, says Heylin, *la bonne bière d'Angleterre* was in great request. Fynes Moryson (1617) tells us that 'the English beer is famous in Netherland and lower Germany, which [beer] is made of barley and hops; for England yields plenty of hops, howsoever they also use Flemish hops. The cities of lower Germany upon the sea forbid the public selling of English beer, to satisfy their own brewers, yet privately swallow it like nectar. But in Netherlands great and incredible quantity thereof is

spent.' The great traveller Fynes Moryson, who here testifies to the Continental triumphs of English beer, may well
have known the James brewery, since his friend Mr.
Walter Wilson, who left him a legacy in 1619, lived at
Puddle Wharf (P.C.C. 5 Soame).

It is a piece of good luck for us that the James brew-
house-cum-dwelling was a 'great' house, and that it stood
on Thames side; for in the views of London in Shakespeare's time, looking north across the water from the
Surrey bank, the water-front is most carefully represented. On examining the crudely drawn 'Ralph Agas'
view of about 1570, we find a large building roughly
sketched on the Puddle Wharf site. But Visscher's view
circa 1616, followed by Merian's, gives an excellent and
realistic picture of the James Brewhouse. It was tall, as
gravitation breweries of any size had to be, and its longer
side stretched north, up Puddle Dock. No doubt the
dwelling-house part of the building was at the northern
end, in Thames Street.

As for the contents of the house we have no details,
but the contemporary inventory of a smaller establish-
ment lists 'a great brewing copper, kettles of copper with
double bottoms, mash tuns or mash fats, wort tuns, under-
backs, gyle tuns, floats, ale tuns, coalbacks' and 'one horse
mill for the grinding of malt.'

This last item, the horse-mill for grinding malt, recalls the Shakespearean term of contempt 'malt-horse'
(*Com. of Errors* 3.1.32, and *Shrew* 4.1.132: 'you whoreson
malt-horse drudge!'). Evidently brewers used old worn-
out hacks for the endless trudging in their malt-grinding
mills. And when Falstaff confesses 'An I have not forgotten what the inside of a church is made of, I am a

peppercorn, a brewer's horse,' he is perhaps more likely to be thinking of the sorry jades that tug in the mill than of the discarded 'great horses' purchased by the brewers to haul their drays: animals which had to have considerable pulling power and some eyesight remaining.

That Shakespeare knew something of the brewers' processes appears from his use of the term 'wort' (the sweet infusion of malt, unfermented beer), in *L.L.L.* 5.2.233; his figure in *Tit. Andron.* 3.2.38, 'tears, brewed with her sorrow, mashed upon her cheeks,' and the paradox in *Lear* 3.2.82: 'when brewers mar their malt with water.' A line in *2 Henry IV* (3.2.282), moreover, suggests that he had been struck with the nimbleness of a workman up under the roof of the brewhouse, rapidly emptying the buckets as they came to the top of the hoist: 'Come off and on swifter than he that gibbets on the brewer's bucket.'

From a Chancery proceeding (*Benson v. James*, C2Jac.I/B8/28) we learn that the James brewery employed several 'beer-clerks' who had charge of the supplies and kept records and accounts of the receipts and deliveries. That some of this was done by 'tally' (the ancient Exchequer system of notches cut across the grain of inscribed hazel sticks afterwards split in two for matching) is indicated by the name Ben Jonson gives to the brewer's clerk he brings into his *Masque of Augurs*:

> *Peter Notch.* I have brought my properties with me, to express what I am; the keys of my calling hang here at my girdle, and this, the register book of my function, shews me no less than a clerk at all points, and a brewer's clerk, and a brewer's head-clerk.
>
> *Groom (of the Revels).* A man of accompt, sir! I cry you mercy.

Slug (*a lighterman*). Ay, sir, I know him a fine merchant of hops, till all hopt into the water.

The vicinity of the James brewhouse was an interesting one. Its neighbour on the east was the mighty and forbidding Baynard's Castle, where Richard Crookback 'took the crown upon him' (see *Rich. III* 3.5.95, 105, and 3.7). Sir Philip Sidney in 1581 addressed a letter 'from Baynard's Castle'; William Lord Chandos lived in it in 1592. In Shakespeare's day its owner was Henry Herbert, 2nd Earl of Pembroke, enemy of Sir Henry Berkeley, the stepfather of Shakespeare's friend Thomas Russell, esquire. The water-gate called Puddle Wharf or Dock which bounded the James brewhouse on the west, and separated it from the Precinct of the Blackfriars, figures in Beaumont's *Knight of the Burning Pestle* (2.6):

Wife. When we had lost our child (you know it was stray'd almost, alone, to Puddle Wharf, and the criers were abroad for it, and there it had drown'd itself but for a sculler) . . .

In 1604 and 1605 there were dangers other than drowning near Puddle Dock and the Blackfriars Playhouse. It is well known that the hottest of the Gunpowder traitors, Thomas Percy, was auditor for his cousin the Earl of Northumberland, who lived in the great Blackfriars house. The entrance to this was under the gate-house later purchased by Shakespeare. And farther down Puddle Dock Hill, and within a few yards of the James brewhouse, Robert Catesby the archplotter lodged in 1604 with one Powell, at the sign of the Green Dragon—today marked by Green Dragon Court, on the Blackfriars side of the street. And there has somehow been preserved a piece of manuscript music, on the back of which stands the scribbled memorandum, 'To aske for Mr Catsbey att the sine of the Gren Dragon.' It is curious to see how magically a stray surviving scrap like this can bring a bit of the London of the Gunpowder Plot to life for us. At one end of an imaginary tether about 150 yards long we see the Children of the Queen's Revels—little eyases—acting in the Blackfriars Theatre, leased to them by Richard Burbage; at the other, the energetic, rich, godly, and celibate Elias James concocting oceans of the best beer; and between them lodges the fanatic plotter, also well known to Shakespeare and his friends Ben Jonson and mine host William Johnson of the Mermaid, preparing an eruption to shake the foundations of England.

JOHN JACKSON AND
THOMAS SAVAGE

IN OUR preoccupation with the chase of Elias James, we have unduly subordinated John Jackson, whose identification was the means of linking James with Shakespeare. We now turn to Jackson, and to Thomas Savage, both of whom were closer to Shakespeare.

To go back a little and recapitulate what is known, we have at least five men sufficiently intimate with Shakespeare to be chosen to act as trustees for him. To two of these, William Leveson and Thomas Savage, Shakespeare and four of his fellows in 1599 granted their half-interest in the ground lease of the Globe, so that the two, by re-granting to them a fifth part each, could turn the players' shares into tenancies held in common. About William Leveson we have already learned a good deal. He was a merchant venturer, an important worker for the Virginia Company, and a leading fellow-parishioner with Heminges and Condell in St. Mary Aldermanbury. [See my *I, William Shakespeare* (1937), 160–163, 219, 231.] But Thomas Savage, his fellow-trustee for Shakespeare and company, remains to be identified.

Fourteen years after the Globe grants, Shakespeare, coming up to London from his home at Stratford, called on three other friends to act as his trustees in his purchase of the Blackfriars Gate-House in Puddle Dock Hill. These were his bosom friend John Heminges, who with Condell preserved many of his plays for us; William Johnson, vintner, who proves to be the host of the Mer-

125

maid Tavern; and finally, John Jackson, the gentleman whom we have begun to investigate.

In exploring two hitherto unknown friends of Shakespeare we have the exciting sense of entering new ground. John Jackson and Thomas Savage. What kind of men were these who knew Shakespeare so well? I cannot say that I have learned much; but to anticipate the beginning made, let me say that they were both north-country men. Savage came from West Lancashire, between Preston and Liverpool, and Jackson from Kingston-upon-Hull, in the East Riding of Yorkshire. This is highly satisfying. Heretofore it has been matter for regret that the two famous counties of Lancaster and York have hardly any place in Shakespeare's biography outside his Histories. Now, however, we can impartially present them with one friend of Shakespeare each. What makes it even better is to find that these sons of England's northern coasts, west and east, were not only not rivals, or indifferent to each other, but intimate friends. In his will, Savage, calling Jackson 'my very loving friend,' appoints him his testamentary overseer.

Savage (born about 1552) was considerably the elder. He was Edmund Spenser's contemporary, about twelve years older than Shakespeare, while Jackson (born about 1574) was ten years the poet's junior, and almost of an age with Ben Jonson and William Johnson of the Mermaid. Both these north-country men prospered in their careers in London, and became men of substance. Savage belonged to the Goldsmiths' Company, which he remembered in his will by legacies of 'one spowte pott of silver white' and £8 for a supper, but no doubt he gained most of his income from his office as one of the sea-coal meters (measurers) of London. He dwelt in the parish next to that of Heminges and Condell, St. Alban Wood Street, for the last thirty years of his life, from about 1580 to 1611. When he made his will (P.C.C. 78 Wood) on October 3, 1611, he owned at least five houses in London, one of which he had bought of his friend John Heminges, who continued to live in it as tenant. He owned another in the adjoining Silver Street (close to Shakespeare's lodging with the French merchant and tire-maker for Queen Anne, Christopher Mountjoy), which after his death Heminges purchased from his son Richard Savage.

All this is interesting as showing Thomas Savage's close connection with Shakespeare, and with Shakespeare's friends Heminges and Jackson. But interest takes a sudden leap when we come upon the following in his will: bequests of forty shillings to 'the poor of Rufforthe' in the parish of Croston (miswritten *Crofton*), Lancashire, 'where I was borne,' and twenty shillings to his cousin, the widow of Thomas Hesketh, of Rufford. Why should the mention by a London friend of Shakespeare's of his native village in far-off Lancashire stir our minds to excitement? The answer lies in Sir Edmund Chambers's paper on 'William Shakeshafte' in his *Shakespearean Gleanings* (1944), and a brief summary in his *Sources for a Biography of Shakespeare* (1946), from which I take the liberty of quoting here.

Noting the traditional report that William Shakespeare left Stratford at an early age, Chambers continues:

It is possible that he is to be identified with a William Shakeshafte, who in 1581 was a player in a company maintained by one Alexander Houghton of Lea in

Lancashire, and was commended in Houghton's will[1] to Sir Thomas Hesketh of Rufford, in the same county. If so, William may have been using the variant of his grandfather's name, which has already been noted. [In Snitterfield records Richard is also sometimes called Shakstaff and Shakeschafte.] Sir Thomas Hesketh had in fact players in 1587, and his relations with the Stanleys, Earls of Derby, make it not unlikely that on his death in or about 1588 Shakeshafte passed into the service of Ferdinando Lord Strange, who himself became Earl in 1593. Of Lord Strange's players there are many records. Through them William may easily have gone on into the London theatrical world . . . where we find in 1592 William Shakespeare, writing probably for Lord Pembroke's men. (*Sources*, 10, 11; *Gleanings*, 52.)

While Houghton does not positively call Shakeshafte a player, we may agree with Sir Edmund that the context makes the assumption at least highly probable. And when we find the player William Shakespeare in 1599 in London choosing as a trustee a man not only from Sir Thomas Hesketh's Lancashire village of Rufford—a speck

---

[1] The passage from Houghton's will (pr. G. J. Piccope, *Lancashire and Cheshire Wills*, ii. 238) is given in *Shakespearean Gleanings*, 52:

(Executed 3 August, proved 12 September, 1581).

Item yt ys my mynd *and* wyll that Thomas Houghton of Brynescoules my brother shall haue all my Instrumen*tes* belonginge to mewsyck*es and* all man*er* of playe clothes yf he be mynded to keppe *and* doe keppe playeres. And yf he wyll not keppe and manteyne playeres then yt ys my wyll that *Sir* Thomas Heskethe knyghte shall haue the same Instrumen*tes and* playe clothes. And I most hertelye requyre the said *Sir* Thomas to be ffrendlye unto ffoke Gyllome and Will*iam* Shakeshafte nowe dwellynge *with* me *and* eyther to take theym vnto his Servyce or els to helpe theym to some good *master* as my tryste ys he wyll.

on the map more than two hundred road-miles from London—but also related to the Rufford Heskeths by marriage, it clearly does not make Sir Edmund's conjectural identification look less interesting. To be sure, we may have here an astonishing coincidence and nothing more. Yet it would be deplorable to leave it without testing the theory further. Perhaps means may be found to follow the clue.

Meantime any conjecture that sees Shakespeare of Stratford a player at seventeen, before he married Anne Hathaway, should take into account the testimony of William Beeston. William's father Christopher Beeston as a young man had acted for some years in Shakespeare's company. In maturity he was a leading manager, and served as an auditor of Heminges's estate. William, who was trained up to the stage, may have seen Shakespeare in his early days. As reported by John Aubrey in 1681, the old man recalled that Shakespeare 'had been in his younger years a Schoolmaster in the Countrey.' This testimony has been variously treated by biographers, according to taste.

May we not go part way to meet Beeston? 'Younger years' does not necessarily mean as young as seventeen. And if we hesitate to make Shakespeare (of whom no record has been found at either University) a licensed and salaried schoolmaster, or even an usher, it may not be unreasonable to picture him as both player and tutor in a wealthy household in the country. Certainly he was capable, like his contemporary Drayton's 'mild tutor,' of reading good old Mantuan, Ovid and Virgil to the young. Drayton's delightful recollection of Polesworth will bear repeating:

For from my cradle you must know that I
Was still inclin'd to noble poesy.
And when that once *Pueriles* I had read
And newly had my Cato construed,
In my small self I greatly marvell'd then
Amongst all other, what strange kind of men
These poets were; and, pleasèd with the name,
To my mild tutor merrily I came
(For I was then a proper goodly page,
Much like a pigmy, scarce ten years of age),
Clasping my slender arms about his thigh:
'O, my dear master! cannot you,' quoth I,
'Make me a poet? Do it if you can,
And you shall see I'll quickly be a man.'
Who me thus answered, smiling, 'Boy,' quoth he,
'If you'll not play the wag, but I may see
You ply your learning, I will shortly read
Some poets to you.'

As a young man of humour and understanding, and a
supreme dramatic poet *in posse*, Shakespeare would make
a rare tutor. And as a player he would command the other
faculty of the schoolmaster, the preparation of school
plays and the training of children in speaking their lines.
One could doubtless turn up many examples of service in
a household in a double capacity. Daniel Rogers, the
linguist, was both steward to Sir Henry Norris and tutor
to his sons. Many of the musicians in the establishments
of the wealthy sustained a dual role, in playing and in
teaching.

It must be recognized that the spiritual courts had the
power, on the presentment of churchwardens, to forbid
anyone unlicensed by the bishop to teach, even in a private house. I subjoin a sample London case (*Cur. Cons.*

Lond. Acts, Bk. 8, 1601, f. 24) concerning William West, aged twenty-two or twenty-three, January 12, 1601/2:

> West, Wm. schoolemaster in Mr Yelvertons house in St Botolphs extra Aldersgate. Presented that he teacheth in Mr Seriant Yelvertons howse and is supposed to preach   Comparuit et interrogatus if he be a minister he sayethe he is & was ordered by the L B of Peterboro' et dominus inhibuit ei both from teaching & vsing his ministrie vntill he be licenced   xij^d dismissed

In cases, however, where the churchwardens did not present the infraction, unlicensed teaching in a private house would presumably go unhindered.

I have run across a fellow-townsman and contemporary of Shakespeare's who unquestionably had been, in his younger years, a schoolmaster in the country (*Cur. Cons. Lond. Respons. Personalia Testium*, 1581–1593, Bk. 3). His deposition is dated May 12, 1589, and I translate the description he gives of himself:

> William Smithe of the parish of Lucton [Loughton] in the county of Essex, schoolmaster, Bachelor of Arts, where he lived for about one year, and before that in the parish of Waltham Holy Cross, where he lived for about one year, and before that in the University of Oxford, where he studied letters for two years. Born in Stretford upon haven in the county of Warwick, aged 24 years or thereabouts.[1]

---

[1] 'Wille*l*mus Smithe *parochi*a de Lucton in Com*itatu* Essex scholi magister in artibus baccalarius vbi habitavit p*er* vnu*m* fere annu*m* et antea in p*a*rochia de Waltham *san*cte Cruc*is* vbi habitavit p*er* vnu*m* fere annu*m* et antea in Achademia Oxonien*si* vbi incubuit *li*teris p*er* duos annos Oriu*n*dus in Stretford vpon haven in Com-*itatu* Warwici etatis xxiiij^{ti} annoru*m* aut circiter . . .'

This description presents some difficulties. To begin with, our Loughton schoolmaster *may* be the unnamed 'fil: Gulielmi Smith als hoode' baptized September 12, 1565 (*Reg. Stratford on Avon*, ed. R. Savage, Baptisms, p. 10); but the only Oxford matriculate of appropriate name, age, and date seems to be a 'William Smythe' described as 'Worc. pleb. f. 18,' from Exeter College, October 11, 1583, who is not listed as taking a degree (A. Clark, *Reg. Univ. Oxon*. II, 129). Perhaps the problem may be solved by comparing signatures.

At all events, here is a 'W.S.,' Shakespeare's contemporary from Stratford, who in his younger years was a schoolmaster in the country about Epping Forest near London. Is he to be identified with Richard Burbage's otherwise unknown friend William Smith of Waltham Cross, gentleman, who on December 28 was present at Holywell when the Burbages' workmen tore down The Theatre? And is it possible that old Beeston unwittingly transferred the youthful schoolmastering activities of this contemporary William Smith of Stratford to William Shakespeare? Like what song the sirens sang, these are puzzling questions.

We have been led pretty far afield, but we began with Thomas Savage. Having established his identity as a London goldsmith and sea-coal meter, native of Rufford, Lancashire, and in the process strengthened an interesting suggestion for Shakespeare's early years, we now turn to a sketch of Savage's and Shakespeare's common friend John Jackson, gentleman.

While I have not yet discovered his paternity, Jackson's connections with Kingston-upon-Hull are evident, both from a number of judicial records and from his will

(P.C.C. 38 Clarke), executed January 26, 1624/5. He leaves £100 marriage portion to Easter White, daughter of John White. This gentleman, chamberlain of Hull in 1598, was an Eastland merchant trading to Prussia, and (with Joseph Field, merchant adventurer and mayor of Hull in 1603 and 1614), as we shall see, a partner of Jackson's in another enterprise. To his wife Jane (formerly the widow of Jacob James) Jackson bequeaths all his houses and lands in Kingston-upon-Hull, with reversion to John Lockwood, and for default to Peter Lockwood, and for default to Easter White, in that order. These Lockwoods also were no doubt prominent in Hull. The city today has a Lockwood Street, a Jackson Street, and a Field Street.

As early as 1601, when he was twenty-six, we find John Jackson, gentleman, purchasing property in the Yorkshire port. John Gregory of Bethnal Green, Middlesex, esquire (perhaps son of John Gregory, formerly mayor of Hull), for £100 sold him three burgages in Whitefriargate, and a tenement with shops in High or Hull Street.[1] And in the same year Jackson testified in a suit between Robert Dalton and John Lyster concerning a debt and land in Kingston-upon-Hull.[2] While I cannot be sure that the John Jackson who, introduced by the great Sir John Spencer, was made free of the East India Company on October 13, 1601, and purchased an 'adventure' of £240 was our man, I think it very likely.[3]

We have already noted that Shakespeare's Globe trus-

---

[1] C. P. 43/74/16; Yorks Tudor Fines, IV, 168.

[2] C24/290.

[3] *C.S.P. Colonial, E.I.Co.*, 128; Court Book I. 77–78.

tee from Rufford, Lancashire, Thomas Savage, in his will of 1611 appointed as overseer 'my very loving friend John Jacksonne'; and that Jackson, as trustee for Shakespeare, in March 1613 took part in the purchase of the Blackfriars Gate-House. In August of the same year his friend Jacob James's will was proved by the relict Jane, whom Jackson married. In September he joined with three leading merchants of Hull—Joseph Field, John Ramsden,[1] and John White—in the leasing, at a yearly rent of £400 for ten years, of the farm of 'all the duties on

---

[1] 'Here lieth the Body of the Worshipful Joseph Field, twice Mayor of this Town, and Merchant-Adventurer, who departed this Life in the true Faith of Christ.

> *Here is a* Field *sown, that at length must sprout,*
> *And 'gainst the rip'ning Harvest's Time break out;*
> *When to that Husband it a crop shall yield,*
> *Who first did dress, and till this now sown* Field;
> *Yet ere this* Field *you see this Crop can give,*
> *The Seed first dies, that it again may live.*

Anno Dom. Decemb. 1627 Ætat. 63.
Sit Deus Amicus
Sanctis, vel in Sepulchris, Spes est.'

Ramsden, 'a pious, learned, and ingenious man,' died in 1637, and was likewise buried in Holy Trinity, Hull, with the following epitaph: 'Here lies the body of the Worshipful John Ramsden, twice Mayor of this Town, and Merchant Adventurer, who departed in the true faith of Christ the xxj December *Mors omnibus communis.*'

I take these inscriptions from Thomas Gent's *Annales Regioduni Hullini* (1735), 31; and will not resist the temptation to include the vigorous paragraph Gent quotes (p. 84) from the 1600 will of the former mayor and merchant William Gee:

'Whereas, in the Scriptures, the Great God has willed by the Prophet, to say to *Hezekiah*, to make his Will, and to put Things in Order, for that he must die; so I do now pray, and humbly beseech the Great God, to confound and destroy all those *Men, Lawyers,* and others whosoever, to the *Devil,* in the *Pit of Hell,* which do, or shall do, or take upon them to alter this my Will, Amen: Good Lord, Amen!'

wines from Spain, Portugal, Candia, and parts of Levant brought into the ports of King's Lynn, Boston, Kingston-upon-Hull, and Newcastle-upon-Tyne.[1] The lessor was Alderman Sir John Swinnerton, sometime Master of the Merchant Taylors Company, Lord Mayor of London, farmer of the Impost of Sweet Wines, and the most considerable fellow-parishioner of Heminges and Condell in St. Mary Aldermanbury.

This close connection of Shakespeare's John Jackson with the magnates of Kingston-upon-Hull proves to be a valuable clue. For when we pick up John Taylor the Water-Poet's genial story of his *Very Merry Wherry-Ferry-Voyage* made in 1622 by inland waterways to York, we discover that the Sculler's 'proved friend' who gave him letters to the Mayor and to Alderman Field of Hull was 'Mr I.I.' Surely this can be no other than Alderman Field's partner, Shakespeare's John Jackson of London and Hull.

Taylor gives a stirring report of the dangerous fifteen miles he navigated—out of his way—'on purpose to see *Hull.*' His wherry ran into heavy weather where Trent disembogues into '*Humber's* churlish streams.'

And there the swift Ebbe tide ranne in such sort,
The Winde at East, the Waues brake thick & short,
That in some doubts, it me began to strike,
For in my life, I ne'er had seene the like.
My way was vp to *Yorke*, but my intent
Was contrary, for from the fall of *Trent*
I fifteene mile went downewards East Northeast,
When as my way was vpward West Southwest.

---

[1] C2 Ch.I/W84/21.

> And as against the Wind we madly venter,
> The Waues like Pirats boord our Boate and enter.
> But though they came in fury, and amaine,
> Like Theeues we cast them ouer-boord againe.
> This Conflict lasted two houres to the full,
> Vntill we gate to *Kingston* vpon *Hull*;
> For to that Towne I had a Prooued friend,
> That Letters did and Commendations send
> By me vnto the worthy Magistrate,
> The Maior, and some of's Brethren, in that State . . .

Enthusiastically detailing his hearty entertainment in Hull, Taylor does not neglect Mr. Jackson's partner:

> On Munday noone, I was inuited than
> To a graue Iusticer, an Alderman,
> And there such Cheere as Earth and Waters yeeld
> Shew'd like a Haruest in a plentious *Field*.

And after acknowledging further handsome hospitality, he concludes:

> But as at Feasts, the first Course being past,
> Men doe reserue their Dainties till the last,
> So my most thankes I euer whil'st I liue,
> Will to the Maior and his Brethren giue,
> But most of all, to shut vp all together
> I giue him thankes that did Commend me thither . . .

Taylor's own gloss to this climax is 'Mr I.I.'[1]

Having thus established John Jackson as the friend of two poets, the imperial Swan of Avon and the humble Sculler of Thames, we should hardly be surprised to find him turning up as one of the 'noble wits' in the 'worshipful Fraternity of Sireniacal gentlemen [*sirena*=

---

[1] *Works* (1630), pp. 11*b* and 12*a*.

mermaid] that meet the 1st *Friday* of every month at the sign of the Mermaid in Bread Street'kept by Shakespeare's other friend William Johnson. This is how Tom Coryate of Odcombe addresses that distinguished company, which included Jonson, Donne, Drayton, Campion, and other poets. To amuse themselves and to please the entertaining Coryate, they celebrated that trudging traveller's exploits in an unprecedented flock of ironical verses, written in nine languages—if we include 'Utopian,' 'Antipodean,' and Macaronic. Dubbing these 'the encomiastick and panegyrick Verses of some of the worthiest spirits of this Kingdome, composed by persons of eminent quality and marke, as well for dignity as excellencie of wit,' the tireless Tom set them in the forefront of his hastily gobbled-up *Crudities* (1611).

At Coryate's request, John Jackson's contribution to the banquet of wit took the form of an egg, filled with riming meat. If learned Tom had strictly followed the model of a classical supper, Jackson's egg would have led all the rest, and the rear been brought up by an apple— *ab ovo usque ad mala*; but the egg is foisted in somewhere in the middle. I supply a representation of it for ocular proof, but for convenience of reading, here it is in more conventional form:

Incipit Ioannes Iackson.

Can it be possible for a naturall man
To trauell nimbler then *Tom Coryate* can?
No: though you should tie to his horne-peec'd Shoes,
Wings fether'd more then *Mercury* did vse.
Perchaunce hee borrowed *Fortunatus* Hatte,
For wings since *Bladuds* time were out of date.
His purse he hath to print what hee did write,
Else who had reade of thee O wandering Wight?

Who else had knowne what thou hast felt and seene,
Where and with whom; and how farre thou hast beene?
Ere thou to *Odcombe* couldst thy Trophyes bring?
Thy hungry prayses in [t]his Egge I sing,
At thy request, else in another fashion
I would haue pointed at thy commendation:
Thy other Heliconian friends bring store
Of Salt, of Pepper, and Vineger sowre,
To furnish thy Italian banquet forth,
Whereby is plainly showne thy wondrous worth.
Feast *Coryate*, feast the world still with thy trauell,
Discharge the Presse, and care not then who cauell.

Explicit Ioannes Iackson.[1]

In this Humpty Dumpty offering, Shakespeare's friend numbers himself among the Heliconians of the Mermaid club, and shows no lack either of wit or learning in his jest upon the scholarly and venturesome landleaper.

Seizing his opportunity to join in the sport, the voluble Sculler promptly came out with his *Laugh and Be Fat*, passing a comment in rime on each dish of verses served up at Coryate's feast of wit. Taylor's invitation to Coryate to consume Jackson's Egg is of interest. He calls it a 'Ginnie Egge.' The only reason I can think of for this refinement is a possible wish to indicate that his friend 'Mr I.I.' had trading ventures to the Guinea Coast:

IOANNES IACKESON

Thou that has trauel'd much from coast to coast,
Come eat this Egge, that is not rawe nor rost:
For like a friend, this man hath plaid the cooke,
And potch'd this Ginnie Egge into this booke.[2]

---

[1] *Crudities* (1611) Sig. h3ᵛ.   [2] *Works* (1630), 76*b*.

Incipit Ioannes Iackson.

Can it
Be poſſible for
A naturall man
To trauell nimbler then
Tom Coryate can? No : though
You ſhould tie to his horne-peec'd
Shoes, wings fether'd more th en *Mer-*
cury did vſe. Perchaunce hee borrowed
Fortunatus Hatte, for wings ſince *Bladuds* time
Were out of date. His purſe he hath to print
What hee did write, elſe who had reade of thee O
Wandering wight? who elſe had knowne what thou
Haſt felt and ſeene, where and with whom; and how farre
Thou haſt beene? Ere thou to *Odcombe* couldſt thy Tro-
phyes bring? Thy hungry prayſes in his Egge I ſing,
At thy requeſt, elſe in another faſhion I would
Haue pointed at thy commendation: Thy other
Heliconian friends bring ſtore of Salt, of
Pepper, and Vineger ſowre, to furniſh thy
Italian banquet forth, whereby is
Plainly ſhowne thy wōdrous worth.
Feaſt *Coryate*, feaſt the world
Still with thy trauell, diſcharge
The Preſſe, and care
Not then who
Cauell.

Explicit Ioannes Iackſon.

Incipit

JACKSON'S EGG
From *Coryate's Crudities*, 1611

Some further details on John Jackson and on others involved in Shakespeare's Gate-House purchase I have relegated to an appendix.[1] That Shakespeare honoured him with his trust and friendship is ample to recommend him to our goodwill and envy, and I prefer to take leave of him in the glorious company to which we have traced him: the sireniacal fraternity of the Mermaid Tavern.

[1] Appendix A, p. 207.

TWO SHAKESPEAREAN 'FIRSTS'

L ESS-KNOWN CORNERS of Elizabethan records often
produce items so strange in their truth as to make
fiction look a fool. Take a sheaf of little-read letters, for
instance. After the full flavours of a feast of sixteenth-
century letters, the fare offered by a modern *biographie
romancée* or novel about the Elizabethans is discouragingly
flat. Where, one asks, is the breath of life, the unpredict-
able authenticity, the cryptic reference, the warm, inco-
herent, and inevitable transactions of the human creature?
From the waxworks of fiction one returns with gusto to
the 'breathers' who had the substantific marrow in their
bones.

Our present material proves once more that the actual
is far beyond imagining. For who could dream that it
would be in a letter from an insane veteran who fought
under Drake and Leicester that we should discover the
earliest quotation from Shakespeare's first printed work,
Venus and Adonis? Or who could fancy that it would be
a jesting postscript written by Elizabeth's Lucifer, the Earl
of Essex, that would give us our first allusion to Falstaff?
Each of these extraordinaries casts its peculiar light, and
we shall take them up separately.

AN ELIZABETHAN MADMAN AND *VENUS AND ADONIS*

What I have here I think is unique: a unique kind of
proof, if such were needed, of the superiority of Shakespeare's England. Reading it, we shall have to admit that

an Elizabethan, even when suffering from persecution
mania, writes a more vivid and poetical letter than we
lesser men can in possession of our wits. Again it is
unique, in that it gives us a new fact on Shakespeare.
You will agree that many modern maniacs have written
on Shakespeare, but not one of them has produced a
single fact. My Elizabethan madman brings out his fact
with the utmost ease, carelessly, an *obiter dictum*. But to
our tale.

A glance through Volume 99 of the Lansdowne Manuscripts in the British Museum shows that, like other magnates, Lord Burghley was not spared letters from un-
fortunates

> ravishéd with bedlamy—
> Fighting with figments and vain fantasies,
> Chimæras or black spirits of the night.

Most striking are the communications here preserved
(ff. 81–87ᵛ) of William Renoldes, a sufferer from persecution mania and religious frenzy, who in 1593 boasts
that in the last seven years he has sent above 200 letters of
complaint and warning to the Queen, the lords, bishops,
and preachers of England, and sown many broadcast in
the principal streets of London. A man of some education,
on his own showing he served in the wars for the most
part of the last sixteen or seventeen years, since he was
twenty: with Leicester in North Holland, with Drake at
Cartagena, 'in flanders, France, Spaigne, and in the Indies.'
His suit to the Queen is 'ether for my pention of 12ˡⁱ
earely, or else some mony to arme & horse me, or else to
imploy me wᵗʰ the charge of a band of foote men wherby
I hope shortly to horse my selfe.' His mania drove him
into wild accusation, railing, and prophecy, but we can-

not pause upon his consequent periods of imprisonment in Newgate, the Tower, and the Marshalsea, or his examination by Lord Buckhurst and Justice Young.

What concerns us is Renoldes's strange notion that the Privy Council caused certain books to be published with a view to luring him into a belief that the queen was fond of him:—

> . . . they pretend to have a great care to helpe me, asthough they would seme to mervell much why I com not a woing to the queene, seing they have taken such great paynes to printe owte her rare vertues & admyrable bewtie, In on booke Intituled awonder decipherid vppon the 12 of *Reuela*. . . . Also in another booke they discryfe a queenes perticuler giftes of nature, as her cristole eyes & every tethe, her red cheekes and chery lipes. . . . Also in a booke that she walked in the feildes to seke me, so disguysed that her one knv her not, I thinck so indede, for she was so disgvised that I knv her not nether. . . . Also wthin thees few dayes ther is a nother booke made of *Venus* and *Adonis* wherin a queene represents the person of *Venus*, wch queene is in great love (forsothe) wth *adonis*, and greatly desiares to kise him, and she woes him most intierly, telling him although she be oulde, yet she is lustie freshe & moyst, full of love & life (I beleve a goodell more then a busshell full) and she can trip it as lightly as a phery nimpfe vppon the sandes and her foote stepes not seene, and much ado wth red & whyte, But *adonis* regardid her not, wherfore she condemnes him for vnkindnesse, thoes bookes are mingled wth other stufe to daesell the matter . . . yet . . . if they colde once move me by ther printed bookes to com to the queene . . . they suppoes it would be there best sporte, for they would then beleve that by ther bookes I conseavid a secret hope of some great love in the queene towards me. . . .

If this were true, it would be one of the queerest uses to which Shakespeare's works were ever put. Poor Renoldes is but mad north-north-west: he can quote his Shakespeare with reasonable accuracy. To be sure, Venus never admitted that she was old, but Shakespeare's

> Or like a Fairie, trip vpon the greene
> Or like a Nimph, with long disheueled heare,
> Daunce on the sands, and yet no footing seene

comes out quite well in his account.

Though he saw through these books, which are but the Council's 'deepe devises of previe scorninges' against him, poor Renoldes is half-persuaded to try what gallantry will do, for in an accompanying letter to Elizabeth he attempts a gay amorous tone, followed, for safety, by a disclaimer:

> But you will not geve it me except I com to you, for you will have some sporte for your mony, By god I swear, I have heard many say you are a mery wench and a very pleasant gentellwoman, full of prettie conseates, But you are so incredulus that I cannot tell what to say to you, And for love, why you are venus her selfe, even agod of love, But I am not so vainely conseated nor vaine gloriouse in my hope, conserninge that wch I have written, and that wch I do wright, nether have I any fantasticall desiares, nor fanaticall Imagenationes, for I know what I do, and I vnderstand what I wright, nether will I be fed any lenger wth eccoes nor aparelid wth shadowes. . . .

Renoldes's distracted mind exhibits the alternations of madness and lucidity. Now he will spread before us the wild poetry and brilliant action of a vision:

... my Running in to the sea to fetch ser franses Drakes Javeling from the serpent and ... my stryking him and made him retyre in agayne, then sir frances Drake and Sir martin furbesher and others beset the serpent wth ther pennases digging and darting at him tell the kilde him. ...

And again, rejected and despised at Court, he can reproduce a painful scene at Westminster with bitter realism:

I did once see a pore woman lie flat aloung wth her fase groveling vppon the ground, w^{th}in the courte gate at White hawle, near to the preaching plase, the wch woman did so rore & cry being strangled wth grefe, that on mowte hear her to charing crose, whearat many nise courtiers made merry pastime.

Venus and Adonis was entered in the Stationers' Register on April 18, 1593, and the unique example in the Bodleian bears the date 1593; but it is uncertain when in that year it was published. Fortunately our madman is exact in his dates. His sheaf of three letters he dates September 21, 1593, and in the course of one of them he writes: 'Now also know this, that this morning being S^{nt} Mathes day and the 21 of September ... 1593 ... this night past being thursday and S^{nt} Mathes eve ...' Consulting the almanac, we find that nothing could be more accurate. Again, he scattered some letters in Newgate Market on a certain day, 'beinge wednesday and the 8th of August 1593.' Right again. Similarly, he knows the very day when Elizabeth took his petition with her own hand in the Council Chamber, 'but the next sonnday folloing 2 yeomen of the garde put me forthe of the courte gate.'

Deaths from the plague began to diminish about the middle of September. The date of his letters, September

21, falls in with this fact, for he writes, 'and whear as god has begune to decrease his plagves & grevious sicnese in and aboute London . . .'

Evidently *Venus and Adonis* had appeared before September 21; and in view of his proved accuracy, I am inclined to accept Renoldes's statement that it had come out only a few days before that date, and the more so because he thought it was published especially for him. The date is reasonable, since, if Richard Field did not hurry the book out in the spring, he would have been discouraged by the summer pestilence.

What became of our literary maniac after he so obligingly dated the publication of Shakespeare's first book for us? Did he cease from troubling the authorities? No; for at the close of 1595 we find the Privy Council ordering the Keeper of the Marshalsea 'to discharge William Reynoldes . . . and to enjoyne him from henceforth not to presume to come within five myles of the Court without speciall license first obteyned of their Lordships.' Did this get rid of him? Again no, for we meet him once more five years later in London, and, as always, walking the streets and writing letters to magnates.

If one walks the streets long enough, one is sure to walk into news. Renoldes not only walked into the most enthralling scene of Elizabeth's reign—the treasonable and abortive Sunday 'hurlyburly' of Essex and his followers— but the frenetic veteran seized his pen and addressed an unsolicited report on two of the rebels to the Secretary, Sir Robert Cecil, as follows:

The cause I write is this, that this day I saw a note of 65 traitors' names, Essex's confederates, in which I missed the names of two men which I saw in the troop which charged my Lord Burghley your brother and the king of heralds in Gracious Street. One of them is called Captain or Lieutenant Orrell, a follower of the Lord Montegle, a most desperate rakehell as lives. He dwells in Grays Inn Lane, a freeholder of 40 l. the year as some say. The other is one which served Sir Philip Sidney, and after waited on the Countess of Essex: he was in the St. Domingo voyage in my company. His father, as some say, was a 'clokemaker' in London. I saw him very quick and nimble with his silver-gilt rapier and dagger drawn, calling here and there to this and that captain and others of their troop to stand and keep together. But Orrell before mentioned, who holds his neck awry, did run and leap in the forefront with Sir Christopher Blunt and Mr. Busshell, their weapons drawn, crying, 'Saw, Saw, Saw, tray, tray'; where I saw Sir Christopher Blunt run a man into the face that his rapier bowed, and Busshell run at my Lord Burghley's footman, and the rest in like manner at divers other, who were hurt.[1]

Its graphic power has naturally made this account a favourite for quotation by historians, quite unaware that the reporter was a religious maniac. Yet what if he was? His obsession did not prevent him from observing closely and reporting accurately. And in a matter like this, or the dates he put on his letters, Renoldes is no doubt more reliable than many of the presumed sane.

THE EARL OF ESSEX AND 'FALSTAFF'

I pray you commend me allso to Alex. Ratcliff and tell him for newes his sister is maryed to Sʳ Jo. Falstaff.

This is news indeed, tacked on to a hasty note on

---

[1] From the copy printed with spelling modernized, *H.M.C. Salisbury Papers* XI (1906), 46.

affairs of state from Essex to Sir Robert Cecil; and it gives us the earliest allusion to Falstaff, a new Shakespearean 'First.' Where was the amusing discovery made? In the Public Record Office, among the uncalendared papers. My invaluable friend Miss Nellie O'Farrell was recently sifting the State Papers, France, with my interests in mind, when in volume 41, folio 192, she ran upon this surprising quarry. The date is between February 25 and 28, 1598, just when the copy of the first part of *Henry IV* was entered in the Stationers' Register, and some time before the publication of the playbook.

What under the sun does it mean? A joke, obviously, and of the same sort that Philip Gawdy treated his brother to in 1601: 'I will wryte you no neues, but that tis sayde my Lady of Lester [Essex's mother] hathe married one of the playing boyes of the chappell.' Essex's bit of fun is directed at some actual person under the unflattering name of 'S^r Jo. Falstaff,' but who is meant by it? And what is the point of saying that Alex Ratcliffe's sister—the beautiful and beloved Margaret Ratcliffe, Elizabeth's favourite Maid of Honour, who never married—is married to this 'Falstaff'? To get into position to catch the point of the jest, it will be useful for us to cast forward and run over the known Essex-and-Shakespeare matters in the years that followed the acting of *Henry IV*.

The next year, 1599, saw Essex on his Irish campaign. And before the ambitious favourite had proved to the world that he was neither an able general nor a man Elizabeth could trust, Shakespeare staged his *Henry V*, voicing the hope of loyal Englishmen for the Earl's return in honour and triumph:

Were now the general of our gracious Empress
(As in good time he may) from Ireland coming,
Bringing rebellion broached on his sword,
How many would the peaceful city quit
To welcome him!

Ere the summer was out, Essex, by what was at the best criminal negligence, and at the worst treason, had made of that hope a mockery. A brief year and a half more brings us to the crisis and catastrophe of February 1601—Essex's own rebellion.

Just before the storm broke, some of Essex's 'men of action' approached Shakespeare and his fellows at the Globe for a special performance of the out-of-date *Richard II*. Though they did not say so, vivid scenes of successful rebellion and deposition were just what these fire-eaters longed to see on the eve of their attempt to seize the Queen's Government. For a guaranteed extra payment of forty shillings, the unsuspecting company put on *Richard II* for them on Saturday, February 7.

Next day Essex and his two hundred malcontents marched into the city. And 'to face the garment of rebellion with some fine colour,' the cry with which the orgulous peer tried to raise London for his *coup* was an hypocritical 'For the Queen! for the Queen!' Naturally the citizens cheered this sentiment, but failed to catch his treasonable drift, even when he added that England was being treacherously sold to Spain. Whereupon he also cried that a plot was laid for his life; and his band strove to clarify his meaning, and to justify their trooping in arms, by shouting to the crowds that his enemies Cobham and Ralegh 'would have murdered the Earl in his bed.' Here names are named, and we get something tangible.

For whether there was any truth in it or not, this rumour of murder reminds us of the bad blood between Essex and Lord Cobham. And it is this red thread of hatred for Cobham that leads us back to Essex's epistolary joke about 'Falstaff.' It is time we glanced at Cobham's relations with Essex, and incidentally with Shakespeare too.

We shall see that Essex's enemy, Henry Brooke, eighth Lord Cobham, ended his life in disgrace; and while he lived he was no ornament to the peerage. He may be introduced by a word or two about his father, William Brooke. This nobleman, the seventh Lord Cobham, had faithfully served Queen Elizabeth as Lord Warden of the Cinque Ports, and for half a year before his death had been her Lord Chamberlain, with control over theatrical affairs and entertainments at Court. It is well known that he did not like the players. That they reciprocated in kind seems indicated by Shakespeare's choice of the name *Oldcastle* for the fat buffoon later changed to *Falstaff*. Since the actual Sir John Oldcastle in the fifteenth century had married into their family, and taken the title of Lord Cobham, this insolent treatment of the memory of their ancestor by the 'abstracts and brief chronicles of the time' must have been resented by the Brookes as a public affront. Could it, moreover, be an accident that in *The Merry Wives*, produced in the spring of 1597, the jealous Ford chose to disguise himself as *Brooke?* Shakespeare's alterations of *Oldcastle* to *Falstaff*, and of *Brooke* to *Broome*, are symptomatic of offence taken, and no doubt deliberately given.

Though the young Lord Cobham was unreliable, ineffectual, a snob, and scoffed at by the friends of Essex for a coward, an 'ignoble nobleman,' and 'my lord Fool,' he had his uses in the political tug-of-war. Elizabeth found him a convenient make-weight in her struggle to keep down the overpeering ambitions of Essex. And Ralegh, to strengthen his own hand for rivalry with Essex, enlisted Cobham in his faction.

Battle over succession to the office of Warden of the Cinque Ports, which was joined while the incumbent, the old Lord Cobham, was still alive, found Essex exerting all his strength to exclude young Cobham, and to obtain the office for his own adherent, Sir Robert Sidney, or, failing that, for himself. Here are the reports by Sidney's agent of Essex's private communications to him. Said Essex:

> I hold nobody so fit for it as [your master]. Neither do I hear that anybody else stands for it but [Henry Brooke, later Lord Cobham], who of all men is the unfittest. And such hath his base villainies been towards me (which to the world is too well known), that he shall be sure never to have it if I can keep him from it.

Moreover, a week later, after it was clear that the Queen was resolved to give the office to Cobham in spite of him, Essex reported what he had said to the other Privy Councillors:

> I made it known unto them that I had just cause to hate the Lord Cobham for his villainous dealing and abusing of me; that he hath been my chief persecutor most unjustly; that in him there is no worth. If therefore her Majesty would grace him with honour, I may have right cause to think myself little regarded by her.

To this, Cobham naturally retorted. 'The Lord Cobham, hearing how disdainfully my Lord Essex speaks of him in public, doth likewise protest to hate the Earl as much.'

This was in March 1597, about a year before the 'Falstaff' letter. Sir Robert Cecil, already Secretary, and obviously soon to succeed his aged father Lord Burleigh as Elizabeth's chief minister, was eagerly courted and cultivated by the contending factions. No doubt Cobham felt he had some advantage here, as his late sister had been Sir Robert's wife. Who should be more favoured than a brother-in-law? On the other hand, Essex, as a favourite and a Privy Councillor, felt himself already a ruler; and while sparing no effort to build his powerful supporting faction, he also lost no chance of impressing Cecil with his grasp of affairs. As the year ended, Cecil was preparing to go to France on an important embassy to Henri IV. Essex saw to it that several of his able friends and adherents offered to accompany the ambassador. Among those permitted to go along were two intimates of Shakespeare's friend Thomas Russell: Russell's half-brother Sir Maurice Berkeley, and his (and Francis Bacon's) friend Tobie Matthew, and also Essex's cronies the young Earl of Southampton, Sir George Carew, and Sir Alexander Ratcliffe. Essex could rely on these three to keep his end up with Cecil. At home, meanwhile, he would show great zeal for government in Cecil's absence, and ply the minister with the Queen's instructions, and lively reports of developments written in his charming vein.

When Cecil was about to take his leave, there was an astonishing exhibition of political rivalry in honouring him with feasts and entertainments. On January 30 we hear that 'my Lord Compton, my Lord Cobham, Sir

Walter Rawley, my Lord Southampton, do severally feast Mr. Secretary before he depart, and have plays and banquets.'

After the ambassador and his retinue had reached Dover, where they were to embark in five ships for Dieppe, they were held for several days, first by a storm, and then by the alarm of a Spanish fleet's arrival in the Channel. Via Essex's galloping posts to Dover, the latter peril brought Elizabeth's command to Cecil to stay, and then a counter-order permitting him to sail. The last of these was sent on February 17; and for a sample of Essex's humorous vein in a postscript, I give the conclusion of it here:

I pray you commend me to my L. of Southampton and Sʳ G. Caro. and tell them I do envy ther ingrossing of all imployments both civill and martiall by land and sea. Heere is one cryed in London of 27 yeares of age, a round man with litle heare of his head and thatt like mosse, faced like a king harry grote, of a sanguine complexeon, and a merry witt. Yf any such be strayed into your company, I pray you have care he be sent back.

It would be interesting to know which of Essex's friends in the party answered to this caricatured description. At all events, the jesting spirit of the postscript prepares us for a similar tone in the 'Falstaff' note, written a week or ten days later, which runs in full as follows:

To my honorable frend Sʳ R. Cecyll principall Secretary and her Majesties Ambassador to the french King.

Sir. I haue newes of this postes going butt att the instant of his departure. I neede say nothing to you of the intercepted letters nor of the Qs directions to you for thatt will appeare by the Qs owne despatch. Butt yf my L. Cobham do butt lett you know thatt which he is wittnes of you shall find I am very honest frend and professe no more then I make good. I wish you all happines and rest

Your affectionate and assured frend
Essex

I pray you commend me to my L. of Southampton and Sr G. Caro. I wrote to them both by one Constance and had written now yf I had any tyme. I pray you commend me allso to Alex. Ratcliff and tell him for newes his sister is maryed to S^r Jo. Falstaff.

The Earl's desire to stand well with Mr. Secretary is evident. He challenges his rival Cobham to bear witness to his honest and active friendship for Cecil. Yet in the same letter he cannot resist a sly disdainful dig at someone known to his friends as 'Sir John Falstaff'; and, as will be seen by what follows, that someone must be Cobham.

For despite a character far from admirable, Cobham was looked upon as a quarry worth the pursuit of marriageable ladies. Was he not a peer, and graced by the Queen with the Wardenship of the Cinque Ports? And was he not closely allied with the all-powerful Cecils? Tongues had begun to wag at least as early as March 1597, when the word went round that he was to marry Lord Oxford's daughter. Nothing came of that, or of a later rumour that he would espouse the only daughter of the sometime Lord Mayor, Sir John Spencer, said to be the richest heiress in England. But the gossips were not discouraged, for meanwhile the field seemed to be narrowing to two chief figures.

The first of these was Elizabeth's favourite Maid of Honour, Margaret Ratcliffe, sister to the gallant Sir Alexander Ratcliffe of Ordsall, a bright star of the Court as much admired for her wit and character as for her beauty. There is no proof that Margaret Ratcliffe went out of her way to charm Cobham, though the magnet of her loveliness was powerful enough to draw any man. But it was well known that Cobham was attracted—sufficiently to give Essex's joke its point; and we see Cobham's enemy chaffing his crony Sir Alexander Ratcliffe with the mock announcement of his sister's marriage to 'Sir John Falstaff.'

The other name most frequently linked with Cobham's was that of the young widow of the Earl of Kildare, Frances Howard, whose father was Nottingham, the Lord Admiral, and whose mother was the Queen's cousin and old companion, Kate Carey. This young lady set her cap at Cobham, and proved persistent and determined in the chase, using her kinship with the Queen to improve her material fortune and to secure the royal support for her claims. As early as January 1599, about a year after the 'Falstaff' letter, the gossips were prematurely expecting a marriage between Lord Cobham and the Countess of Kildare. Cobham, however, had no intention of marrying her unless her portion were considerably increased; and the Queen seemed unwilling to grant his terms.

In the spring of this year Essex went off on his Irish campaign, and with him went the Earl of Southampton and Margaret Ratcliffe's brother as colonel of a regiment of foot. Cobham, who liked danger about as much as he liked Essex, of course stayed at home. Yet while delaying marriage for pecuniary reasons, he was not above finding solace elsewhere. And the result of his looseness appears in the gossipy postscript to a letter from the Countess of Southampton (found and published in the 1870's, and written, as Mrs. C. C. Stopes discovered, on July 8, 1599) to her son in Ireland. For here we find 'Falstaff' again; not married, to be sure, but confidentially presented by his mistress with spurious young fry:

> Al the nues I can send you that I thinke wil make you mery is that I reade in a letter from London that Sir John Falstaf is by his Mrs Dame Pintpot made father of a go[o]dly milers thum, a boye thats all heade and veri litel body, but this is a secrit.

Who was Cobham's mistress and secret love, here equated with 'good pintpot, good ticklebrain' Nell Quickly? We are not told. Yet on pursuing the little fish called 'miller's thumb' we are exhilarated to discover what no Elizabethan eye would miss: the sly mental play on 'Cobham.' For the other common name for that small-fish-with-a-big-head (*Uranidea gobio*) proves to have been *cob*. '*Cob*, a fish, also called a miller's thumb' (Webster). '*Bózzolo*, a fish called a millers thomb or a cob' (Florio). '*Cobbo*, a miller's thumb' (Grose). We may now be confident that the news which will make Southampton merry is that 'Sir John Falstaff'—Cobham—has a clandestine little Cob.

It is clear enough that although *Oldcastle* had long given way to *Falstaff*, the new name clung to Cobham as the old had done, despite Shakespeare's careful disclaimer in the Epilogue to the second part of *Henry IV*, 'Oldcastle died a martyr, and this is not the man.' But the

Countess of Kildare was determined to marry Lord Cobham, and cannot have relished the public ridicule of her intended. Might not something be done about it? Her father, the Lord Admiral, had a troupe of players, chief rivals of the Shakespeare company. Could not they procure and put on a play to rehabilitate the memory of the martyred Oldcastle, the 'good Lord Cobham'? Such an effort might possibly lay the mischievous ghost of Oldcastle–Falstaff. The galled jade Cobham may have suggested the idea himself; or the Countess may have thought of it, and to please Cobham persuaded her father to give an order to his players.

However it began, we have the result, an attempted counterblast: a piece of dramatic hackwork by Drayton, Mundy, Wilson, and Hathwaye, called *The True and Honorable Historie of the Life of Sir John Oldcastle, the Good Lord Cobham*. Its prologue takes a wooden moral tone, and begs a favourable hearing for the 'truth' as against the beguiling false invention of Shakespeare:

> It is no pampered glutton we present,
> Nor aged counsellor to youthful sin,
> But one whose virtue shone above the rest,
> A valiant martyr, and a virtuous peer . . .
> . . . let fair Truth be graced,
> Since forged invention former time defaced.

Could this attempt have had any popular success in the face of Falstaff's tremendous vogue and the notorious character of the living Lord Cobham? I doubt it. And when we are told by the manager Henslowe that on the occasion of its first performance, November 1599, the company gave the playwrights ten shillings 'as a gefte,' I suspect this was rather a share of a gratuity from the Countess of Kildare than any symptom of large gate-receipts. Moreover, though we know that the play was completed in two parts (to match *Henry IV*), there is no sign that the second part ever reached the stage.

. . . . .

In *Henry V* (1599) Shakespeare brought his imaginary Falstaff to a sad end. But the real lives of these whom we have seen stirred to jest by the thought of the fat knight were also touched by tragedy. The same summer brought a 'very foul' defeat to Essex's troops in Ireland, and his gallant friend Sir Alexander Ratcliffe 'bravely in the battle fell and died.' Though Ratcliffe was but twenty-five when he was killed, the French ambassador wrote to Henri IV from London that he and Sir Conyers Clifford, who fell with him, 'sont regrettez icy comme les meilleurs hommes d'Angleterre.' Margaret Ratcliffe had already lost one brother in Ireland; and the news of Alexander's death, though Elizabeth herself broke it to her as gently as she could, struck a blow at her heart. From that moment she pined, refused food, and a few weeks later she died. Ben Jonson's feeling epitaph spoke the universal love and sorrow:

*M*arble, weep, for thou dost cover
A dead beauty underneath thee,
*R*ich as nature could bequeath thee:
*G*rant then, no rude hand remove her.
*A*ll the gazers on the skies
*R*ead not in fair heaven's story
*E*xpresser truth, or truer glory,
*T*han they might in her bright eyes.

> *R*are as wonder was her wit,
> *A*nd like nectar ever flowing,
> *T*ill Time, strong by her bestowing,
> *C*onquered hath both life and it:
> *L*ife, whose grief was out of fashion
> *I*n these times. Few have so rued
> *F*ate in a brother. To conclude,
> *F*or wit, feature, and true passion,
> *E*arth, thou hast not such another.

Early in 1601 Essex went to the block as a traitor; and his ally the Earl of Southampton was fortunate to have his own death sentence commuted to perpetual imprisonment. After years of false alarms, our precious Cobham at length married the Countess of Kildare in the spring following Essex's execution; but very soon infuriated her father, Lord Nottingham, by rejecting his bride. The contemporary news item reads, 'The Lo: Cobham hath put away his goodly Lady, whereat the Lo: Admyral ys much offended & they two great enemyes.' The accession of James brought Southampton's release from prison; but shortly thereafter Cobham, accused of seditious plotting and attainted of high treason, was stripped of his offices and property, degraded from the Order of the Garter, and in his turn imprisoned in the Tower.

In sum, our new 'Falstaff' allusion from the pen of the Earl of Essex not only underlines the one we already had from the Countess of Southampton, but also reveals that the latter likewise refers to Cobham. And though these jests were tossed off as trifling merriments, a pursuit of them draws us into the high and moving drama of Elizabeth's England.

For Shakespeare's part in the story, these Falstaff=

Cobham jokes show that despite his changing of *Old-castle* to *Falstaff*—and we have seen that the altered name was firmly fixed in the minds of Essex and his friends by the beginning of February 1598—the enemies of Cobham were not at all disconcerted by the change. 'Falstaff' was as good a stick to beat him with as 'Oldcastle' had ever been. We owe the Earl of Essex something for giving us the earliest allusion of any kind to Shakespeare's greatest creation in comedy. And as for Falstaff himself, his first appearance offstage and outside a book is in a jest, quite in character: for he is 'the cause that wit is in other men.'

'NOT OF AN AGE'[1]

'HE WAS not of an age, but for all time.' Ben Jonson's praise of Shakespeare remains the most precious of all. It is not only the verdict of a great scholar and an honest and severe critic, but that of a jealous artist, competitor, and intimate friend: one of those rare contemporary judgments that stand the test of centuries. 'He was not of an age' means that he was not a mere period-poet, an innovator, the source of a peculiar Elizabethan literary influence. Misled by this quality (or lack of quality) in Shakespeare, recent criticism has tried to persuade us that he was not a representative Elizabethan. For example, Professor Tucker Brooke, while emphasizing Shakespeare's genius, wisdom, and insight into character, points out quite rightly that he 'was not the advanced political thinker that Bacon was, or Ralegh, or Spenser, or even Marlowe'; that his patriotism was Tory, feudal, not expansionist or imperialistic, his religious outlook archaic; that he remained a stranger to the tremendous intellectual currents of his day. Professor Brooke concludes that 'the student of Shakespeare will know much of human nature, but not a vast deal about the sixteenth-century mind.'

I accept Professor Brooke's arguments and disagree with his conclusion. What was the sixteenth-century mind, and who represented it? The Bacons, Raleghs, and Spensers were exceptional thinkers, outposts, explorers, leaders; and as such of course not *representative* of any-

---

[1] From an address delivered at the Folger Shakespeare Library, Washington, D.C., April 23, 1940.

thing but their own extraordinary selves. Obviously, to find out the characteristic thought of an age you don't go to startling innovators, but to the average man, *l'homme moyen sensuel*, the man who feels and acts intuitively, and distrusts intellectualism. And Ben Jonson, although he knew that Shakespeare was not even, like himself, the inventor of a new type of drama, nevertheless went on to recognize him for what he was, the *essential Elizabethan*, and to hail him as the 'Soul of the Age.' The soul is the immortal part. Ben Jonson did not have to be reminded that social doctrine, political theory, advances in science, economic or geographical expansion, and altered church government are unimportant influences in the life of the soul. He knew that what does matter is the conscience and the heart: man's most intimate relations with himself, his fellows, and his God. Death, love, hate, sin, repentance, courage, fear, compassion, cruelty, forgiveness, revenge, joy, grief: it is about these things in himself that man does most of his thinking, under the stimulus of emotion; and he does it in terms of the prevalent morals, assumptions, and prejudices of his day. His thinking is not logical, systematic, speculative, or scientific. To a professional thinker it is not thinking at all. But it is unquestionably the only vital thinking that is done, and its quality and character constitute the mind of the age. Through his dramatic poetry, in a variety of fascinating and often heroic figures, Shakespeare interpreted his age to itself.

'He was not of an age, but for all time,' is Ben Jonson's prophecy. A century and a half rolls away, and another sovereign of the realm of letters, Dr. Samuel Johnson, in his tribute to Shakespeare, bears witness in noble words to the truth of the prophecy:

The poet [writes Dr. Johnson] of whose works I have undertaken the revision, may now begin to assume the dignity of an ancient, and claim the privilege of established fame and prescriptive veneration. He has long outlived his century, the term commonly fixed as the test of literary merit. Whatever advantages he might once derive from personal allusions, local customs, or temporary opinions, have for many years been lost; and every topic of merriment, or motive of sorrow, which the modes of artificial life afforded him, now only obscure the scenes which they once illuminated. The effects of favour and competition are at an end; the tradition of his friendships and his enmities has perished; his works support no opinion with arguments, nor supply any faction with invectives; they can neither indulge vanity, nor gratify malignity; but are read without any other reason than the desire of pleasure, and are therefore praised only as pleasure is obtained; yet, thus unassisted by interest or passion, they have passed through variations of taste and changes of manners, and, as they devolved from one generation to another, have received new honours at every transmission.

Here is praise, consummate because uttered by a great man. And if Dr. Johnson had lived to our times, he would have seen no reason to qualify it. But what of that interesting passage, 'his works support no opinion with arguments, nor supply any faction with invectives; they can neither indulge vanity nor gratify malignity'? Dr. Johnson would open his eyes to read that in Nazi Berlin Prince Hal was run through the propaganda machine, and emerged as certified Grade A pap for Hitler Youth. Shakespeare's notion of the divine right of kings came out altered as the latest brand of *Führerprinzip*. In Moscow, Dr. Johnson would be treated to the spectacle of citizen-

producer Popoff grappling with the problem of Bol-
shevizing *Romeo and Juliet*. 'Naturally,' confesses Com-
rade Popoff, 'my first step was to consult the Communist
Academy and the Marx–Engels–Lenin Institute, because
the sole way to understand this genius's strength and
weakness is by determining his revolutionary class atti-
tude.' Shakespeare triumphs over barriers of time and
language. His appeal overleaps even the prison-walls of
totalitarianism, and calls so strongly to the people's
hearts that the masters of propaganda dare not shut it out.
They imagine that all will be well if they are careful to
interpret him to the credulous populace with their
customary lie.

To reflect on such treatment of Shakespeare is an expense of spirit in a waste of shame. But when we rise
above this morass into the realm of literature, and consider serious critical interpretations, we often find something instructive that exhibits the critic very clearly, but
leaves Shakespeare untouched. Thus, that incisive thinker
Mr. T. S. Eliot is on very strong ground when he points
out the misleading nature of criticism of *Hamlet* by minds
naturally of the creative order. Goethe, he reminds us,
made of Hamlet a Werther. And Coleridge turned him
into a Coleridge. Quite so; but when he himself ap-
proaches the question of Hamlet, Mr. Eliot challenges
judgment on the very ground he took to warn us away
from those dangerous fellows, Goethe and Coleridge.
And if we find him presenting us with a highly modern,
frustrated, and Freudian Hamlet, we shall have to look it
over very carefully before accepting it. What then *is* Mr.
Eliot's *Hamlet*?

Well, after mentioning the basic Hamlet-saga and the

surmised but non-extant earlier play, he notes that Shakespeare added to it the absorbing theme of anguished son
and guilty mother. Mr. Eliot concludes that 'Shakespeare's
Hamlet, so far as it is Shakespeare's, is a play dealing with
the effect of a mother's guilt upon her son, and that
Shakespeare was unable to impose this motive success-
fully upon the intractable material of the old play.' Mr.
Eliot's corollary is therefore that *Hamlet*, however 'great'
it may be, is an artistic failure. To his mind, Shakespeare
planned to make this added theme of mother-and-son the
central interest of his play, and was defeated.

Here we have the critic assuming that he knows what
Shakespeare was trying to do, which is something he cannot know. And of course until you know what the intention was, you cannot pronounce on success or failure
in execution. Are we to conclude that the mother–son
motive was meant to be the core of Shakespeare's *Hamlet*
merely because it was the motive which Shakespeare
added to the old theme? This hardly follows. Would it be
safe to conclude, because Shakespeare supported his
treatment of the Lear story by adding Sidney's parallel
theme of the prince-with-two-sons, that therefore the
latter took first place in Shakespeare's mind as the central
interest or core of his play? Finally, we may question the
notion that an unsuccessful treatment of the mother–son
motive is really the significant matter in Shakespeare's
Hamlet, if we are asked to believe that the play has had
to stagger misunderstood through three centuries of universal acclaim while waiting for the epoch of Professor
Freud to find out the truth about it.

No; appreciation and criticism of Shakespeare in
modern times and from a modern point of view may com-

pletely miss the mark. And here I must reluctantly pick another bone with Mr. Eliot, whose thought usually commands my admiration. He is speaking of Ben Jonson, but what he says may apply to Shakespeare as well:

> We must see him [says Mr. Eliot] unbiased by time, as a contemporary. And to see him as a contemporary does not so much require the power of putting ourselves into seventeenth-century London as it requires the power of putting Jonson in our London.

Now what does this mean? To my mind there are only two ways of seeing Jonson as a contemporary. We must either look at the world of art from his point of view, or make him look at it from ours. The latter course is impossible. Unless you take the trouble to become deeply versed in the terms of thought and the essential spirit of the time in which Jonson was formed, and whose idiom he spoke, it is useless to talk of having the power of putting him in modern London, for what you put there won't be Jonson.

A leading humanist and authority on Renaissance iconography, Dr. Erwin Panofsky, has succinctly stated the problem.

> The humanist, [he says] dealing as he does with human actions and creations, has to engage in a mental process of a synthetic and subjective character: he has mentally to *re-enact the actions* and to *recreate the creations*. It is, in fact, by this process that the real objects of the humanities come into being.

This is well said. If I may risk a rather lame metaphor from Ben Jonson's trade, the humanist in imagination

takes up the bricks for himself and lays them to understand how the splendid Renaissance structure was put
together. But first he must know the composition,
strength, size, shape, and colour of the brick, and the contemporary methods of laying and bonding.

Similarly, in the case of a more or less ancient author
(Shakespeare, for example), intelligent saturation in his
works is not enough. The preliminary task is to pene-
trate into the basic mental attitudes of his time, to find out
what he might have meant *then*, and to ascertain the
probable value he attached to his meaning. The poet
Rupert Brooke was well aware of the position. As he says,
'a good Elizabethan play is a play that would have been
good in Elizabethan times; and not a play that is good to
us, with our different ideas. The two categories coincide
to a great extent. But their differences are important.' He
is right; and to determine these differences, we must
attempt to perceive the quality and force of the connota-
tions that clustered about the Elizabethan words. A word
never stands alone. Its cloud of associations is ever
shifting, evaporating, re-forming. Take, for example,
the word *communism* today. What we need to know is
the state of mind or quality of emotion produced by the
word.

Only by a long apprenticeship to the thought and external life of the Renaissance is the student of the humanities or of Shakespeare progressively fitted for his task.
Only by serving that apprenticeship does he grow less
liable to gross misinterpretation of our author. Shakespeare's fellow-dramatist Tom Nashe shows, in a vehe-
ment passage, how real the danger was, even with contemporaries. Here are Nashe's words:

Aretine, in a comedy of his, wittily complaineth that upstart commenters, with their annotations and gloses, had extorted that sense and moral out of Petrarch, which, if Petrarch were alive, a hundred strappadoes might not make him confess or subscribe to. So may I complain that rash heads, upstart interpreters, have extorted and racked that unreverent meaning out of my lines, which a thousand deaths cannot make me e'er grant that I dreamed of.

In our day we talk a great deal, and very enthusiastically, too, about the Elizabethan age. With us Americans it is a delighted and proud ancestor-worship. But we are human, and fall into the facile subjective error of praising Shakespeare's age only for the qualities we fancy in ourselves. Thus, we extol the Elizabethan youthful vitality, the nation's zest in pioneering enterprise; we share its pride in prosperity and new-found importance in the family of nations, and approve the opportunities for initiative and ambition that resulted in the rise of the middle class. There is no harm in this, and it is valuable if it increases our intelligent interest in Shakespeare's background.

Yet while rejoicing in these undeniable affinities with the Elizabethans, we must not forget the many differences between their outlook and ours. Shakespeare's contemporaries read a very popular book called *Seven Sobs of a Sorrowful Soul for Sin*. They bought up edition after edition of *The Sick Man's Salve*, and of *The Pensive Man's Practice*. An Oxford scholar, Mr. John Higgins, brought out a best-seller called *An Answer to Mr. William Perkins concerning Christ's Descension into Hell*. Shakespeare could pick up a copy of Friar Bartholomew

On the Properties of Things, a standard authority on Natural History, and perhaps read the following note on beans: 'Beans cause vain dreams and dreadful; by oft use thereof the wits be dulled . . . Therefore the Bishop should not eat Beans.' In a case of domestic difficulty, he could look up an approved recipe in Albertus Magnus as follows:

> That a woman may confess what she has done. Catch a live water-frog, and take out its tongue, and put the frog back into the water, and put the tongue over the region of the woman's heart while she is asleep, and when she is questioned, she will tell the truth.

Guiding its precarious political life England had an able ruler; and she was a woman, every inch a queen, who read Plutarch and Sophocles in the original Greek, and could converse fluently in several modern languages, as well as in the diplomatist's Latin. A story goes that on a visit to Winchester College, Queen Elizabeth asked one of the boys (in Latin, of course) whether he had been whipped recently? The answer came promptly, in the rueful words of Aeneas to Dido: '*Infandum, regina, iubes renovare dolorem.*'

In a competition with us in the Fine Arts, the glorious Elizabethans could even leave Shakespeare *hors concours* and still win hands down. Two obvious proofs of their superiority spring to mind. First, their frequently demonstrated power, unknown in our age, of marrying the two high arts of lyric poetry and music. As Peter Warlock put it, the Elizabethan composer was able 'to recreate the full beauty of the poet's thought in music.' There was even that rare spirit, the poet-composer. Thomas Campion, in setting his own poems to music, tells us, 'In these English ayres, I have chiefly aimed to couple my words and notes lovingly together, which will be much for him to do that hath not power over both.'

The other proof is, of course, the unmatched poetry of their drama. The most penetrating word on this central Elizabethan mystery of dramatic poetry is that of Mr. T. S. Eliot: 'What makes it most dramatic is what makes it most poetic. . . . This is not by a concurrence of two activities, but by the full expansion of one and the same activity.' To illustrate this power of theirs—impossible to define—the Elizabethans would not need to call in Shakespeare. They could give you a passage such as this from Marlowe:

[*The ruthless Tamburlaine replies to the plea of the captured virgins for mercy. He is about to order his lancers to slaughter them*]

Tamb.   Behold my sword; what see you at the point?
Virgins. Nothing but fire and fatal steel, my Lord!
Tamb.   Your fearful minds are thick and misty, then;
         For there sits Death; there sits imperious
             Death,
         Keeping his circuit by the slicing edge.
         But I am pleased you shall not see him *there*;
         He is now seated on my horsemen's spears,
         And on *their* points his fleshless body feeds.

And one more, from *The Duchess of Malfi*. Here John Webster with one stroke takes us into the tortured mind of a murderer:

How tedious is a guilty conscience!
When I look into the fish-ponds in my garden,
Methinks I see a thing armed with a rake
That seems to strike at me.

Dramatic poetry is not only a Shakespearean power; it is an Elizabethan power. Any attempt to isolate Shakespeare is not only futile; it is dangerous. It has been well said that we must know all of Shakespeare's work to know any of it. In the same sense it is true that we must know all the Elizabethans in order to know Shakespeare. We must know the Elizabethan life in order to know Shakespeare's life, and for Shakespeare a vital part of that life was the mental powers of his audience.

It is a truism to say that a work of art must comprise three elements: the artist or author, his medium, and the recipient. On the whole we have not chosen to admit to ourselves what the phenomenon known as Elizabethan drama proves about its recipient, the Elizabethan audience. Everyone recognizes the existence of three kinds of audience. There was first the exclusive and brilliantly dressed gathering of royalty, nobility, and courtiers at a command performance at Whitehall. Next there was the select audience of courtiers, lawyers, students, and wealthy townsfolk at the indoor, so-called *private*, theatres, such as the Blackfriars. Finally, there was the large and very mixed crowd at open-air or *public* playhouses like the Globe—some courtiers in the lord's rooms, some inns-of-court gallants smoking on stools on the stage, citizens and their wives in the galleries, and a turbulent press of nutcracking, apple-chewing groundlings or 'understanders' in the yard—handicraftsmen, watermen, apprentices.

Shakespeare and his fellow-dramatists sometimes addressed themselves more particularly to one or another of these three audiences, but most of the plays could not afford to be caviare to the general. *Hamlet*, for instance, philosophical and 'literary' as it is, is known to have pleased all, high and low. Now if one thing is clear, it is that the English drama developed and improved in Shakespeare's lifetime; which proves that these audiences were accustomed to receive it so attentively and appreciatively that the playwrights were encouraged to refine their style. And it was these audiences, groundlings included, whose minds were so alert, whose senses were so quick, that they savoured and applauded the phenomenally rich and supple metaphor, the sudden shifts of meaning, the rapid-fire plays on words of men like Marlowe, Jonson, and Shakespeare.

If we accept the findings of modern psychology when it asserts a positive correlation between vocabulary and intelligence, what answer can we make? Their vocabulary was, of course, different; but it was undeniably larger, too. We are forced to conclude that the Elizabethans were more intelligent than we are. Our playwrights cannot command, our audience cannot cope with, a comparable wealth of language. There is no way round it; words correspond to ideas; they had more words and quicker wits. Of course we squirm, and say that their puns and conceits are overdone, and constitute a blemish; the fact remains that playing with words is a proof of energetic wit and literary ability. We disapprove when they descend to rant and huff-snuff rhetoric. Our censure would be more honest if we could rant half as well.

An admission that Shakespeare's audiences were our mental superiors is a bitter pill. Let me give an example of the lengths we will go to in refusing to swallow it. Not long ago I watched a leading Shakespearean scholar wrestling with the question. Confronted by the intricate

and swiftly moving jests, clenches, and wit-combats in
Shakespeare's comedies, many of which we today must
painfully puzzle out in the study, he simply could not
believe that Shakespeare's audience could catch and follow them at the speed of performance. Though he made
every allowance for their familiarity with a vocabulary
and an idiom which are often strange to us, he still thought
it quite impossible. His despair at last drove him into
absurdity: he concluded that the spectators carried
memorandum-tablets to jot down the passages they failed
to understand, and went home to study them out! What
can we say of the mental power shown in producing a
theory such as this? Like every playwright, Shakespeare
wrote to be understood, understood at high speed; and
he *was* understood. If his hearers had failed to understand,
he had two obvious alternatives: (*a*) to simplify his language, or (*b*) not to write at all.

Humility is perhaps a novel mood for us, but a touch
of it will do us no harm. We don't dare patronize the
Athenians of the Age of Pericles: we know them for our
masters. We daren't call *them* quaint, superstitious, or
backward. The Elizabethan world was more spacious than
ours; why? Because their morality had little room for
hypocrisy; because their life embraced unafraid traffic
with painful emotions, that is, with passions. Unable to
reduce or control physical suffering, they had to face the
worst. Consequently education of children was severe,
and they were taught not to fear the hardships of life, and
to tackle them young. Their way of meeting life sharpened
their senses, quickened their wits, and gave them a grasp
of human experience that we can only envy.

It is impossible to follow the thoughts and actions of so

great a people even imperfectly and by fragments, and not to benefit greatly by them. Do you wonder, then, that I regard the time well-spent which I have passed reading the writings and the life-records of the Elizabethans who called Shakespeare their own? Of course, like other enthusiasts, I have been trying in the process to add something, however small, to the poet's biography; but it is naturally only once in a great while that one can discover a document which in the narrowest sense is a new fact about Shakespeare. Throughout the search, however, the countless other Elizabethan circumstances have been creating a mental climate or landscape. That landscape is some insurance against unconscious distortion or unwarrantable treatment of such a discovery. The new-found fact must find its proper harmonious place in the picture.

Better than by these generalities I can illustrate what I mean by taking you with me in pursuit of a specific detail about Shakespeare. We have so few such details to work with that we cannot afford to be careless with them. You read detective fiction, and know that every trifling detail must be regarded as important until its insignificance can be shown beyond a doubt.

Now, the only externally documented view we have of the poet domesticated, or *Shakespeare intime*, is the one discovered more than thirty years ago by Professor Wallace, which shows him as a valued lodger in the Silver Street house of the Huguenot French 'merchant stranger,' Christopher Mountjoy. You will allow that as a lodger he behaved sympathetically. For at the request of Mrs. Mountjoy, Shakespeare persuaded the apprentice Stephen Bellott, 'a very honest and good fellow,' to marry Mary, the daughter and sole child of the house. Why it was necessary to call in the world's greatest dramatist as a matchmaker is not made clear. Possibly Mountjoy had not offered a marriage portion sufficient to tempt Bellott, who had ideas of setting up for himself, and needed capital. In any case, that question does not concern us here.

The detail we shall pursue is the art, craft, or trade of Shakespeare's landlord, Christopher Mountjoy. In the legal documents he is described as a *tiremaker*, which in Elizabethan lingo means a maker of head-dress for ladies. Good! Now please observe what happens to Elizabethan ladies' head-dresses when modern scholars and professors—mere men—get their hands on them. Sir Sidney Lee, to begin with, defines *tire* correctly as ladies' head-dress. But then Mountjoy's address, Silver Street, catches his eye, and his literary mind recalls a passage in Ben Jonson, in which Captain Otter very villainously traduces his own wife's beauty, as follows: 'All her teeth were made in Blackfriars, both her eyebrows in the Strand, and her hair in Silver-street.' Not being prone to see double meanings, Sir Sidney did not understand *Blackfriars*, *Strand*, and *Silver-street* to imply that her teeth were *black*, her eyebrows mere *strands*, and her hair *silver-white*; he took it merely, and no doubt rightly, to mean that these were the places where she bought spare parts.

Now mark the mental process. Mistress Otter bought her false hair in Silver Street. *Argal*, she bought it at Mountjoy's. Again *argal* (though I shudder to say it), ladies' head-dresses are wigs. O most lame and impotent conclusion! Mind you, Lee doesn't *say* all this; but if he didn't mean it, why did he illustrate Mountjoy's trade with the passage about hair being bought in Silver Street? Next we come to our friend, Dr. Joseph Q. Adams. Dr.

Adams stands by himself as the only biographer who has proved equal to treating Shakespeare's stay in the French household with imagination. He gives us a charming suggestion of the poet taking little lessons in conversational French from Mary Mountjoy, like those in *Henry V*. But having said this much, we are compelled to admit, with sorrow, that after explaining *tire* as head-dress, Dr. Adams speaks in the next paragraph of Mountjoy's as a *hairdressing* shop, and also quotes that horrid passage about hair bought in Silver Street.

Yet he is by no means the worst. Exhibit C is Professor Tucker Brooke, who bluntly describes Mountjoy as a 'French Huguenot tire-maker (wigmaker).' Here we have it without any decent reticence. To Professor Brooke, a tire, or ladies' head-dress, is a wig. The last stage in this *débâcle* is that represented by Professors Neilson and Thorndike, and Hardin Craig, who quietly and utterly *suppress* the beautiful Elizabethan word *tire*, and bring Mountjoy before us as a 'wig-maker' and nothing more. But in their defence these gentlemen may urge that a wig-maker is better than nothing. True. Professor Mackail, in his *Life of Shakespeare*, starves us outright. He leaves Shakespeare's landlord without a trade, a street, a Christian name, or even a nationality—'one Mountjoy,' he says, 'in Cripplegate.' Mackail is the complete butcher of this struggling little fact about Shakespeare.

Now let us go back to Shakespeare, at the height of his best productive years, looking for rooms. From what we know of him, I ask, is it likely that from among the hundreds of available furnished lodgings, he would deliberately choose a room at a wigmaker's? Choose to live in an aura of unfortunate creatures coming to sell the glory of their womanhood, and others, certainly less attractive, coming to buy that hair made over to give them a false beauty? Would he willingly seek out a climate heavy with hair-oil, hot irons, crimping, and curling? Was it in an atmosphere of this kind that the greatest English dramas were written? Let us appeal to Shakespeare himself on the matter. We find that he rarely mentions wigs; and when he does so, it is usually with aversion or contempt.

In *Love's Labour's Lost*, Berowne says that his lady's brows mourn

> That painting and usurping hair
> Should ravish doters with a false aspect.

Worse, such adscititious tresses were often taken from the dead. Shakespeare stigmatizes the practice in three striking passages:

> So are those crisped snaky golden locks
> Which make such wanton gambols with the wind,
> Upon supposed fairness, often known
> To be the dowry of a second head,
> The skull that bred them, in the sepulchre.
> (*Merch. of Venice* 3.2.92–6.)

> Before the golden tresses of the dead,
> The right of sepulchres, were shorn away,
> To live a second life on second head;
> Ere beauty's dead fleece made another gay.
> (Sonnet 68.5–8.)

> *Timon* (to Phryne and Timandra):
> and thatch your poor thin roofs
> With burdens of the dead; some that were hang'd,
> No matter; wear them, betray with them, whore
> still.
> (*Timon of Athens* 4.2.145–7.)

And as for men's wigs, who does not recall Hamlet's disgust at the 'robustious periwig-pated fellow'? No; Shakespeare was an actor, and could not avoid wigs in the theatre, but he certainly did not like them on women's heads.

Let us put the whole subject of wigs as far away as possible. Banish periwigs, perukes, and false hair. Return to tires, and we shall vindicate Shakespeare's taste and the adornment of Elizabethan ladies.

Actually their head-dresses were marvellous confections of gold, pearl, and precious stones. The foundation was a coif, caul, hair-net, or hair-lace cunningly woven of gold thread, in or on which jewels were mounted. One of Queen Elizabeth's tires was 'a Jewel, being a ship of Mother-of-Pearl, garnished with rubies.' And in Montemayor's *Diana* we have this: 'The attyre of her head was in form of two little ships made of emeralds, with all the shrouds and tackling of clear saphyres.' Falstaff has such ornaments in mind when he flatters Mistress Ford that she is beautiful enough for a royal court: 'Thou hast the right arched beauty of the brow,' he assures her, 'that becomes the ship-tire, the tire valiant, or any tire of Venetian admittance.' The tire-maker's and wire-drawer's art came to France and England from Venice. Sea-borne commerce and sea-power were the life-blood of both Venice and England. The ship was their symbol and palladium. No wonder their ladies wore ships on their heads.

These rich head-dresses frequently inspired the poets in their singing of love and beauty. Thomas Morley, for example, set the following canzonet to music:

In nets of golden wires,
With pearl and ruby spangled,
My heart entangled
Cries out and help requires.

Sweet love, from out those briars
But thou vouchsafe to free me,
Ere long alive, alas! thou shalt not see me.

And Thomas Bateson composed a madrigal to a lyric
which begins:

Have I found her (O rich finding!),
Goddess-like for to behold,
Her fair tresses seemly binding
In a chain of pearl and gold?

In planning and executing these forms of beauty,
Christopher Mountjoy was an artist and craftsman: a
kind of lesser Benvenuto Cellini, the kind of man Shakespeare would choose for a landlord. In a lawsuit I discover him described as one who practised the art or
mystery of making and working gold and silver thread,
'commonly called Venice gold and silver thread.' Shakespeare knew this precious material well, and refers to it in
The Taming of the Shrew: 'Valance of Venice gold in
needlework.' And in 1620 I find Stephen Bellott, Mountjoy's former apprentice whom Shakespeare helped to
matrimony, complaining to King James. He says that for
many years he has got his living by working gold and
silver thread, but that recently the servant of a monopolist
of the trade searched his house, broke open a door,
and carried away his mill, the only instrument of his
living.

A subordinate part of the mystery of gold and silver wire-drawing was what was called 'spinning upon silk,' or intertwining the threads of gold or silver with the silken strands. At Mountjoy's Shakespeare must have seen Mary at this beautiful work, and he readily uses the technical term:

> Be't when she weav'd the sleided silk
> With fingers long, small, white as milk . . .

This couplet from *Pericles* may well be a memory of Silver Street.

If we remember Shakespeare's familiarity with wefts of gold and nets of silver prepared from coin and bullion in Mountjoy's workroom, we shall perhaps understand how he obtained a metaphor which otherwise seems far-fetched:

> Here lay Duncan,
> His silver skin lac'd with his golden blood.

While *silver* and *golden* here furnish a mere impression of the *colour* of the king's skin and shed blood, they carry a powerful suggestion of their *preciousness*.

When rich silks were heavily stitched or brocaded with gold thread, the result was called cloth of gold. Fabric woven of gold thread on a light foundation of silk was called *tissue*. Tissue paper got its name from being laid between folds of gold fabric, or tissue, to prevent fraying. In all Shakespeare, perhaps the most gorgeous picture is Enobarbus's description of Cleopatra's barge:

> She did lye
> In her pauillion, cloth of Gold, of Tissue. . . .

The line as printed in the Folio sets off *cloth of Gold* from

the capitalized word *Tissue* with a comma.[1] The sense
therefore is two fabrics; not only cloth of gold, or bro-
cade, but also tissue, fabric almost all of gold: the richest
of all weaving, and the kind that Shakespeare could see
taking shape under deft fingers at Mountjoy's.

So much for what we have discovered of Mountjoy's
art. His *clientèle* was diverse. No doubt he supplied gold
thread and the less sumptuous tires to the travelling merchants or peddlers who frequented country fairs. What
would you find in the pack of Autolycus?

> *Golden quoifs* and *stomachers*
> For my lads to give their dears.

> Any silk, any *thread*,
> Any *toys for your head*
> Of the newest and finest?

The gentry went to Mountjoy to adorn their ladies.
Here is a letter, dated 1594, from the wealthy East An-
glian gentleman Philip Gawdy:

> I have sent my well beloved syster all such things
> as she requested, her fann with the handle, not stale
> any kynde of waye [that is to say, the latest thing in
> every respect]; a payre of knyves; a vardingale of the
> best fashion; her gold thread, her heare call [hair caul];
> her pumpes; and in short there wanteth nothing she
> spake for, but only a thing I should have had of Mr.

---

[1] That *cloth of gold* and *tissue* were two distinct fabrics, as the
Folio punctuation indicates, is attested by Anthony Jenkinson, in
his description of the rich robes of Ivan the Terrible: 'gownes . . .
of rich tissue and cloth of gold . . .'—Hakluyt, *Principal Naviga-
tions* (Everyman ed.), I. 428. And by Spenser: 'All ouer her a cloth
of state was spred, Not of rich tissew, nor of cloth of gold.'—
Faerie Queene, 5.9.28.

Munjoye, but he fayled me very wrongfully according to his promyse; but it is coming.

The 'thing' was no doubt a tire, or head-dress. You notice that although Mr. Gawdy is annoyed by the artist's common fault of promising more than he can perform, he nevertheless respectfully calls him *Mr.* Mountjoy—a strong hint of the position the Frenchman held in the world of London. He is found elsewhere described as a *merchant stranger*, and I have a document showing that he was an importer of materials from abroad.

To cap this I have found evidence of his eminence still more striking. It is contained in the accounts of King James's Queen, Anne, for the year 1605. Along with payments to the jeweller royal, we find the audit of the account of 'Marie Mountjoy tyrewoman.' Mrs. Mountjoy is the only tiremaker I have found in the surviving accounts. The amount of her bill for tires for the Queen was fifty-nine pounds—say from $400 to $500 in our values. Part of it was paid on November 17, 1604, two days before the wedding of her daughter Mary Mountjoy to Stephen Bellott, the marriage which Shakespeare had brought about.

We have acted on the principle I am emphasizing, namely, the fullest use of the Elizabethan background, and the detail we began with has brought us to a minor climax. We have found that the Mountjoys were no ordinary tiremakers, but of the best in London. They made head-dresses for the Queen. Mrs. Mountjoy must have discussed the proposed tires with her royal majesty, received the jewels to be incorporated in them, and later helped to show her how they were to be worn.

We are now equipped to make a visit in imagination to Silver Street, say early in October 1604. What shall we find in the busy household of Christopher Mountjoy? In the shop and workroom, glittering with silk, Venice gold and silver thread, jewels, and tissue, the best hands and brains, including those of the young lovers, are active, preparing a rare ornament for the head of the Queen. Upstairs, their friend Shakespeare is hard at work on a tragic tale of lovers, finishing *his* Venetian offering for the Queen, *Othello, The Moor of Venice*.

By November 1, he and his company are ready, the fresh lines all learnt, and present the new play before James and Anne and their brilliant court in the Banqueting House at Whitehall. Perhaps at the performance the Queen is wearing the new Mountjoy head-dress. Four days later Shakespeare and his fellows are again before royalty, this time with the revived *Merry Wives of Windsor*, in which, as we have seen, Falstaff assures Mistress Ford that she is beautiful enough for a royal court: 'Thou hast the right arched beauty of the brow that becomes the ship-tire, the tire valiant, or any tire of Venetian admittance.' Within two weeks the Queen has paid Mrs. Mountjoy a large part of her bill, and thereupon the marriage of the two young fellow-craftsmen, prepared by Shakespeare, takes place.

We know that Shakespeare was lodging with the Mountjoys in this year of 1604, and must already have been intimate with them for some time to be called upon to make up a match in the family. In 1612 he testified that he had known them for ten years or so, which takes us back to 1602. Now a further fact comes to light. When we look at Christopher Mountjoy's will, made in 1619, we

are fascinated to find that Mountjoy was also intimate with
the circle of Shakespeare's fellow-players, Heminges and
Condell, to whom we owe the preservation of the plays
in the First Folio, for Mountjoy's will was witnessed by
John Heminges's son-in-law, and by an important trustee
of Henry Condell's wife's.

We have come to the close of our little hunt, which
began with a revulsion from wigs, and ends with the First
Folio. Of course, we are not trying, by new biographical
details, to solve the insoluble mystery of poetic genius.
But the more we can learn of the life that Shakespeare
knew, the truer will our understanding be of the poetry
which was written in terms of that life.

MOVING TALES are told of the discovery of fact couching unsuspected in the jealous corners of History. Every truly gentle reader shares the finder's thrill, and echoes his ill-suppressed *Eureka!* Yet almost equally engaging is that rarer labour, the task of uncovering the sense of a common little phrase or by-word, whose meaning has unaccountably baffled all attempts at interpretation, whether by critics, lexicographers, or crystal-gazers. And there is a special charm when the phrase happens to be one employed by Shakespeare, and falls from the lips of his Mercutio: Mercutio, certainly a poet, and endeared to us as the most sportive of wits and most fearless of friends. Make no mistake: when a phrase of the keen Mercutio's is low-rated by the foxes of philology as a 'mere quibble' 'of small meaning,' good grapes are being ignorantly miscalled, and it is time to rise in his defence. You can count on it that beyond all obvious quibbles Mercutio means more than some of us suppose.

What then is this expression of his over which we have universally stumbled? It looks ridiculously simple: 'Dun's the mouse, the constable's own word.' But it is no longer simple when one asks, just exactly what does it mean? To begin with, let us see how Mercutio brings it in. Romeo, groaning conventional love for the unseen Rosaline, is begging off from joining in the masquers' dance at the Capulets', where (though he doesn't know it) he will find his true love. Mercutio, sure that dancing is just what he needs, labours to put some heart into him. But Romeo is melancholy, old, and weary. He will stand by with the other gaffers.

> *Rom.* A torch for me; let wantons light of heart
> Tickle the senseless rushes with their heels;
> For I am proverb'd with a grandsire phrase:
> I'll be a candle-holder and look on;
> The game was ne'er so fair, and I am done.

If he were as dull as Jonson's Crispinus, Mercutio might take up this puling Romeo with 'Tut, tut! Abandon this idle humour; 'tis nothing but melancholy.' But Mercutio's efficient touch is lighter. Snapping up Romeo's last word, with its neat double play on *done* (finished, done for) and *dun* (dark, not *fair* like *the game*), he instantly converts it into a triple:

> *Mer.* Tut! Dun's the mouse, the constable's own word!
> If thou art Dun, we'll draw thee from the mire
> Of this sir-reverence love . . .

Mercutio's third sense is 'Dun'—the proverbial name of the dark-coated reliable nag, the good old horse whom all would turn out to help if he were bogged down: the horse who gave the name to the old Christmas horseplay of 'Dun's in the mire.'

All this is clear, but what of 'Dun's the mouse'? What is that mouse doing there? Well, the learned men who have grappled with the phrase gravely inform us that it means 'The mouse is brown.' Surely a pronouncement straight from the kindergarten, unworthy of a Mercutio still in petticoats; and hardly a message apt to cheer a love-sick Romeo. No. We must not take the phrase by the wrong end. Mercutio didn't say, 'The mouse is dun.' Hold on to the horse. In Mercutio's mouth 'Dun' is not the adjective colour, but the good old substantive horse, Dun. He's the mouse. But can a horse be called a mouse? Why not? On the home stretch, if he looks like winning, he has even been called a sweetheart, a baby, a honey-child. And to Shakespeare (see *Hamlet*), 'mouse' means 'darling,' 'jewel,' 'best one.' Indeed, as a common term of endearment in Elizabethan English, 'mouse' is often applied to a man—a husband or a crony. In *Westward Ho*, Mistress Wafer tells her husband, 'Your flesh and blood is very well recovered now, mouse.' And Judith Honeysuckle, who has a cold, asks her husband, 'Mouse, what's good for't?' In *The Woman Hater*, Julia coaxes Lazarillo with, 'Come, mouse, will you walk?' And in *The Roaring Girl*, Tearcat summons his pal Trapdoor with, 'Let us go, mouse.' Finally, Mistress Snore, in *The Wits*, tries to make her husband, Constable Snore, desert his beat by this touching plea: 'Truly, my mouse, I cannot sleep without thee.'

With the mouse established as the darling, favourite, or best one, we return to the woeful Romeo, offering Mercutio his quantum of quibble in the sigh, 'The game was ne'er so fair, and I am done.' And now we can savour the force of Mercutio's cheering retort: 'What if thou art Dun? That's nothing to moan about. Tut! Dun's the darling, as the constable says. Old Reliable; and well worth rescuing. If thou art Dun, we'll draw thee from the mire, and get thee out of this bog of love.' No nonsense or mere quibbling in Mercutio.

Now, allow for the sake of argument that we have here succeeded in running down both Dun and the mouse in *Romeo and Juliet*. Remains a third unknown—the constable. How and why is 'Dun's the mouse' *the constable's own word*, as Mercutio says? To solve this one we had better look a little farther into the proverbial reputation of Dun. We soon find his sterling qualities admired far and wide among the common people. And he endears himself especially by combining sturdy reliability (on which the folk pride themselves) with an exterior unpretentious, homely, plain, and dull-coloured—like their own garb. In *Oldcastle*, the Hostler affectionately asks the Carrier, 'How does old Dick Dun?' adding, 'He has been ever as good a jade as ever travelled.' Galloway, that corner of Scotland famed for sturdy nags, contributes a hearty rhyme about him:

'The eel-backit din
Ne'er laes his master far ahin'.'

Eelbacked refers to the black stripe in the coat of some duns—the *fauveaux à la raye noire* of Rabelais. In Russia, Dun is called *Burka*; and they say there, '*Harashó na búrku valit*' . . .' 'It's all right to pile it on to Dun; Dun'll carry it all away.' If you chose to take the trouble, you could no doubt find praise for him in the popular by-words of most of the languages of Europe. He might even turn out to be the 'dark' horse of the race-track!

The common folk-notion which emerges from the praise of the dun nag is something like, 'Put your money on the plain, dark, homely chap. He's the sure card. He'll see you through. Dun's the mouse.' This brings us back to the connection of Dun with the Elizabethan constable. The constable was an ordinary citizen, elected for a year's duty as the parish peace-officer. He had a staff of office—a 'ward staff'—but no uniform, and discharged

his duties in his plain, dull-coloured clothes. Nevertheless he took a reasonable pride in the load of responsibility he carried for his sovereign and his neighbours;
as much as to say, 'I'm not much for show, but you can
rely on me.' Who would more naturally appropriate the
proverb, 'Dun's the mouse' for a motto? Not only constables (as Mercutio tells us), but also sergeants-at-the-
mace disguised in buff seized on it, as we find in *Westward Ho*:

> *Honeysuckle*: Sergeant Ambush, as thou'rt an honest
> fellow, scout in some back-room, till the watchword be
> given for sallying forth.
> *Ambush*: Dun's the mouse. (*Exit*).

Our formula for the meaning of the phrase seems to work
in *Westward Ho* as well as it did in *Romeo and Juliet*, and
Mercutio is vindicated. Still there are several other amusing passages in Elizabethan plays where the proverb pops
up to challenge us. Let us see how the formula fits with
them.

In *Oldcastle* we have a scene from the Lollard rebellion.
'Plain William' Murley, the brewer of Dunstable (*quasi*
Dun's stable?), is mustering his irregular band of knaves
armed with skulls, leather jacks, and spears—

> John and Tom and Dick and Hodge,
> And Rafe and Robin, William and George—

as they come on the stage, 'prepared in some filthy order
for war.' Plain William looks them over. Weapons rusty.
No uniforms, scarlet or otherwise. No feathers for their
steel caps. Assorted dress of the plainest and homeliest.
In short, a ragged regiment. But what though? Dun's
the mouse! And so he tells them:

Come, my hearts of flint, modestly, decently, soberly, and handsomely, no man before his leader. Follow your master, your captain, your knight that shall be, for the honour of meal-men, millers, and malt-men. Dun is the mouse. Dick and Tom, for the credit of Dunstable, ding down the enemy tomorrow. . . . I would give a couple of shillings for a dozen of good feathers for ye, to set ye out withal. Frost and snow! A man has no heart to fight till he be brave.

So much for the bold brewer. He is confident that the finely dressed enemy will learn to their cost that Dun's the mouse.

When we come to *The Two Merry Milkmaids*, we find the scene laid in a court glittering with courtiers as brilliant outside as they are dull within. But two of the ladies, the Duchess Dorigene and her friend Julia, brimful of gay wit and satire, are contemptuous of the shallow brains of these silken water-flies. They lay a plot to dress up (or rather, down) as humble homespun milkmaids, and in that plain disguise to get the laugh on the courtiers with some home truths. Here is another chance for ' Dun's the mouse,' with a quibble as well, for the showy courtiers will be 'undone':

Dorigene. . . . I have a great mind to jeer the courtiers.

Julia. Prythee let's. There requires not much wit about it.

Dor. Is't done?

Jul. If my consent will do't, 't is.

Dor. Why then 't is done; and Dun's the mouse, and undone all the courtiers.

. . . and like milk-maids will we go, To make sport with the courtiers, and triumph.

In the next sample Babulo, the clown in *Patient Grissil*, is recalling the routine difficulty they meet with in getting him roused out of a morning:

> *Bab.* 'What, Babulo!' say you. 'Here, master!' say I; and then this eye opens; yet Dun is the mouse—lie still. 'What, Babulo!' says Grissil. 'Anon,' say I; and then this other eye looks up, yet down I snug again.

How does what we now know of the meaning of 'Dun's the mouse' apply to Babulo's babble? Perhaps he is making a disparaging contrast between his bright (open) eye, which couldn't sleep through the first show-a-leg summons, and the dusky (shut) eye, which could be counted on to stay asleep longer, and thus prolong his rest. Since that better eye is dusky or dun, Dun's the mouse; and half-asleep is better than broad awake.

There is no uncertainty in the last case to be examined —a passage from one of the plays wrongly attributed to Shakespeare, *The London Prodigal*. It is a scene of family grief. Sir Lancelot Spurcock's fairest and most witty daughter, Luce, has ruined herself by flouting her father and all her friends in marrying a wild-oats, a libertine, a prodigal. The father is burdened with his load of sorrow. But Civet, a plain, steady young man who marries the unpretending and not-too-clever daughter Frances, says what he can to console him:

> *Sir Lancelot.* Son Civet—daughter Frances—bear with me;
> You see how I am pressed down with inward grief
> About that luckless girl, your sister Luce . . .
> *Civet.* Father, 't is so, 't is even fallen out so; but what remedy? Set hand to your heart, and let it pass. Here is your daughter Frances and I; and we'll not

say we'll bring forth as witty children, but as pretty
children as ever she was, though she had the prick and
praise for a pretty wench. But, father, Dun is the mouse.
You'll come?

Sir Lancelot. Ay, son Civet, I'll come.

By quoting 'Dun's the mouse,' Civet clearly means
'though your fair and witty daughter has gone the wrong
way, we plainer, more homely ones are to be relied on.'

What a pity that this muscular little phrase of Mercutio's
could not have survived into modern use! Proverbs such
as 'Fine feathers make fine birds' and 'Handsome is as
handsome does' in comparison strike feebly on the ear.
But I hold to a sneaking hope that a racy current equiv-
alent of 'Dun's the mouse' exists in full force and virtue
somewhere in the language. Who will tell me what it is?

THE ADVENTURE OF THE
SINGLE RAPIER

ONE MAY as well confess that, in the hands of a cunning literary craftsman, the theme of Murder as one of the Fine Arts attracts us more than we care to think about. Of even the best morbidity, a little goes a long way. With zest, therefore, a healthy mind turns to Detection of Crime, where obscure and imaginative killings are purely by the way, and the chief fascination grows from the enthralling processes of the detective mind. The sovereign power of this interest makes itself felt in the Mousetrap play-within-the-play of *Hamlet*. Here the Murderer, pouring the liquid poison into the Sleeper's ear, pours a shudder into us; but from this we are lifted at once to the crest of excitement by the detective glance with which the prone Hamlet pierces the heart of Claudius.

Now, although I listen like a three years' child to tales of the amazing achievements of those geniuses Sherlock Holmes and Philo Vance, I cannot down a grudging sense of their good fortune. Lucky fellows, I say, to be furnished with a supply of selected crimes, carefully committed for them to solve! For a literary detective is denied the advantages of a detective in literature. No omniscient author predigests his problem, carries the answer up his sleeve, and provides the puzzle with fascinating varieties of circumstance. True, the Case of Christopher Marlowe came pretty well within the regulations. One knew that the poet had been killed, and the puzzle was to find the slayer and throw light on the crime. But there are cases

in which we must begin with far less hope of success—
cases in which we are completely in the dark.

For if the lost crime was committed upwards of three
hundred years ago, and no one has heard of it from that
day to this, your detective faces a sporting proposition.
He must begin sans newspaper, sans confidential in-
formant, sans everything but his curiosity. In two words,
he must start from scratch; and it is to the story of such a
novel hare-and-hounds that I now invite you.

Henry Porter, you must know, is an arresting presence
in the stormy procession of Elizabethan dramatists—no
less arresting because he vanishes so suddenly and
strangely from our sight. First mentioned in Henslowe's
Diary, in December 1596, as one of the leading and popular playwrights for the Admiral's company, he runs for
two years and a half thereafter a lively career—writing
three plays himself and collaborating in two others. In
one of these he worked with Ben Jonson: a significant
association, for the two must have had much in common.
Like Jonson vigorous and downright, he further shares
with Ben the distinction of introducing the amusing
'humour' or type character to the English stage. And more
than this can be said for Porter on the authority of his *Two
Angry Women of Abingdon*, the only play of his that has
come down to us. Unlike Jonson's, Porter's genius was
pure English, uncomplicated by Renaissance influence
and borrowing. His people are drawn from nowhere but
the life of the English countryside; their shrewdly observed characters are richly developed in a hearty
humour and a plain and flowing English. Francis Meres
placed Porter in a group with Shakespeare as 'the best for
Comedy amongst us.' *The Angry Women* may stand

shoulder-high to *The Merry Wives*. Here is no space for an adequate appreciation of Porter's genius. There is keen regret for his lost plays. Havelock Ellis well says, 'Many golden galleons of our drama lie sunken at the bottom of the sea; few that we would more gladly recover than the stout oak-built ships of Harry Porter.'

Natural enough, we may say, to expect the loss of many an Elizabethan playhouse manuscript. Plays in any age are mostly fugitive productions. But the unexplained disappearance of a leading playwright is another matter—one which sets the curiosity ablaze and the hounds of the imagination straining in the slips to be off on the trail of the lost Harry Porter.

The most insatiable of clue-hunters would find food for his hunger in Chancery Lane. Here in the Record Office are thousands and tens of thousands of parchment rolls and files of documents from Elizabeth's England. In such a *matto grosso* the great question is, of course, which way to turn first, which of the countless jungle tracks to follow.

For a hint, let us look to the last known trace of the missing man, found in Henslowe's *Diary*—an acknowledgment written in his own hand: 'Be it knowne vnto all men that J henry Porter do owe vnto phillip Hinchlowe the some of x^s of lawfull money of England wch J did borrowe of hym the 26 of maye a° dom 1599. Henr [*sic*] Porter.'

Now Henslowe, as everyone knows, lived in Southwark—Southwark, that turbulent transpontine appendage of London which harboured the Bear Garden and Henslowe's Rose Theatre. In Southwark, too, were brothels—the notorious 'stews' of the Bankside, near the elegant town house or palace of their landlord, the Bishop of Winchester; prisons—the King's Bench, the Clink, the Marshalsea, and the White Lion; alehouses—three hundred of them; courts of justice—Southwark Assizes and the High Court of Admiralty, both held in St. Margaret's, a disused church which also housed the jail called the Southwark Compter. A catalogue grim enough, exhibiting a very Elizabethan mixture of religion and crime.

This whole congeries has long disappeared from the face of Southwark. But in the Record Office documents are to be found which bring it to life for us. If we dip into the criminal files of the High Court of Admiralty, for instance, we find the sea-thieves and murderers haled before their judges in St. Margaret's Church. Pirates on trial for their lives a bowshot from the Bankside stage where Shakespeare is acting with his fellows! The temptation to digress is too seductive, and I am absorbed to find interesting proof that the Admiralty had cognizance of crimes committed not only on the high seas but on the London Thames as well. Here we find a specimen—the murder of a waterman, one of the fraternity of Taylor the Water Poet, by a dangerous religious maniac:

John Lawson, late of London, yeoman, came running along the street in Redrith and called for a pair of oars; and the said John Staples, now dead, and William Aide took him at Redrith Stairs into their wherry; and as they rowed him from the Stairs towards London, the said John Lawson began to read on a Bible which he had in his hand, and said the devils and witches had bewitched him and brought him that day out of his chamber; and being warned by the water men to call upon God, he read on his Bible again; and, looking up again, he said he thanked God he had, and [He had] saved him from them. And then he, the said John Lawson, of a sudden, in the said wherry in the river of Thames over against St. Saviour's Mill, within the jurisdiction of the Admiralty, the said fourth day of April aforesaid, being devilishly minded, drew his rapier and thrust the said John Staples through the neck on the right side, and also into the thigh ten inches deep up towards his body, and hurt him also in the left hand in two places; of which wounds so given . . . the same Staples languished about the space of half an hour, and then died.

With stories like this coming before my eyes, it is difficult to put aside the Admiralty records, though, to be sure, they are hardly likely to contain a clue to the vanished Henry Porter.

But a better source suggests itself—the Southwark Assizes. Southwark was in Surrey in those days, and Surrey came under the South-Eastern Circuit. Here luck is with me, for of all the records of the Clerks of Assize preserved in the Record Office the only ones which extend back into the sixteenth century are those of the South-Eastern Circuit. I promptly send for a bundle, and, on opening it, select the Surrey file.

Here before me on the old brown slips of parchment are lists of the justices of jail-delivery, panels of jurors, and quantities of original indictments—indictments for petty larceny, for non-attendance at church, for witchcraft, for assault, for seditious speeches, for highway robbery, for manslaughter, for murder. Is the lost playwright to be found among them? Hunting fever is growing on me as I grope my way along through that grim wood where on every second tree a felon hangs.

I reach the file for 1599, the year of Porter's disappearance. Is my quarry here? The leaves of parchment fall swiftly . . . strange names flit past . . . and now, Porter. Henry Porter. Killed. Is this my man? The date—June 6. Eleven days after he disappeared from Henslowe's book. The missing playwright is found; and his tragic death is told in a legal Latin which may be Englished as follows:

SURREY: The Jurors for our Lady the Queen present that John Daye, late of Southwark, yeoman, on the sixth day of June in the forty-first year of our Lady Elizabeth by God's grace Queen of England, France, and Ireland, Defender of the Faith, &c., with force and arms, at Southwark aforesaid in the said county, not having God before his eyes, but moved and seduced by the instigation of the Devil, *of his malice aforethought feloniously* made an assault upon a certain Henry Porter, and when the said Henry then and there was in God's peace and the peace of the said Lady the Queen, with a certain sword, *Anglice* a rapier, of the value of two shillings, which the same John Daye had and held in his right hand, feloniously struck, then and there giving to the same Henry Porter a mortal wound on the left breast of his body of the length of one inch and of the width of one inch, of which mortal wound the said Henry Porter languished at Southwark aforesaid in the said county, from the said sixth day of June in the forty-first year aforesaid until the seventh day of June then next ensuing; on which seventh day of June in the year aforesaid, at Southwark in the said county, the said Henry Porter died of the said mortal wound. And thus at Southwark in the said county the said John Daye, in the form and manner aforesaid, *of his said malice aforethought* feloniously killed *and murdered* the said Henry Porter, against the peace of the said Lady the Queen, her crown and dignity.

The first thing to note here is that the inquest jury brought a charge of murder against the slayer. But the passages I print in italic were subsequently struck out; and on turning the parchment over I find the endorsement of the grand jury: 'Not found for murder. True bill for manslaughter.' Furthermore, over the name of John Day at the head of the indictment the clerk has entered a memorandum of the trial and verdict: 'Puts himself guilty; no goods; self-defence, and he fled to a certain wall beyond which, etc.'

While this is formal language, the meaning of it is clear enough. Day confesses that he killed Porter. 'No goods' means that he has no property to be forfeit to the Crown for his felony. He urges self-defence in extenuation of his crime, offering evidence that he retreated as far as possible from Porter—or, in the old phrase, he 'fled to a certain wall, beyond which he could in no wise go without peril of his life'—before defending himself effectively with his rapier. On referring to the docket of prisoners at the bottom of the file, I find Day's name, with the note 'gave bail for next, etc.'—which is to say that he found sureties for his appearance 'at the next jail-delivery in his proper person to plead his pardon or yield his body to the order of the Court.' Day, then, was released on bail, and, since his name does not appear in the record of the following jail-delivery, we must conclude that, like Ingram Frizer, he was granted a royal pardon for homicide in self-defence.

With this account we may contrast Ben Jonson's trial at Middlesex Sessions in the preceding year for killing the actor Gabriel Spencer in a duel. Unlike Day, Jonson is presented, not for murder, but for manslaughter. At his trial he has no evidence of self-defence to offer, and to escape the gallows which awaits the convicted felon he pleads clergy: 'He asks for the book, reads like a clerk, is marked in the hand with a T, and is delivered according to the form of the statute.'

In spite of the expense involved in securing a pardon, Day got off better than Ben Jonson. For not only is it painful and ignominious to be branded in the hand, but such a mark is a distinct disadvantage. If you should happen to kill another adversary, no amount of clerkly scholarship would save you from the tree. Benefit of clergy could be claimed once, and no more.

But we have got ahead of our story. Who was this John Day, at whose hands Harry Porter had his last quietus? The question answers itself. Who should he be but the rival playwright for Henslowe's company, John Day, who collaborated with Chettle in *The Blind Beggar of Bethnall Green*? What more natural than a heated quarrel between two men employed by one manager, especially between two playwrights, who, according to the *Diary*, never collaborated with each other? Further evidence is given by Ben Jonson himself, who, a month before he killed Gabriel Spencer, had collaborated with Porter in the play, *Hot Anger Soon Cold*. A fellow worker with Harry Porter, Ben was no friend of Day's, and in conversation with Drummond he calls Day 'rogue' and 'base fellow.'

These are hard words for admirers of Day's work to swallow; and we have no other testimony than Ben's as to his character. What can be said of his writings? Of his plays, perhaps the most characteristic is *Humour out of Breath*. Here, though to be sure in a less delicate form, we find the 'polish and politeness,' the wit and Arcadian grace, of *Love's Labour's Lost* and *As You Like It*. Further, *The Blind Beggar of Bethnall Green* shows that on demand Day could collaborate in producing boisterous and bustling scenes of realism and crude humour with some indifferent success. But, left to its own pleasure, Day's talent found its most grateful path to expression in the poetry of his delightful *Parliament of Bees*. Of this sweet fancy Charles Lamb wrote:

> The doings,
> The births, the wars, the wooings

of these pretty little winged creatures are with continued liveliness portrayed throughout the whole of this curious old drama, in words which bees would talk with, could they talk; the very air seems replete with humming and buzzing melodies while we read them. Surely bees were never so berhymed before.

But we must leave the measuring of poets' fame to Time's yardstick, and return to the dark business with which we began. Who can say with any confidence what provoked the quarrel, and how the playwrights fought? Except for the certainty that Day thrust Porter into the breast with a rapier, we are in ignorance. No further light comes to us from either combatant, whether from Porter's twenty-four hours of languishing life or Day's remaining years.

A fancy strikes me that perhaps Porter lacked Day's skill with the rapier. To many an untravelled Englishman it was still a fairly new weapon, and Porter's play shows its author English to the core. Is there a trace of Porter's own feelings in the words he puts into the mouth of the humorous serving man Dick Coomes?

Nay, mistress, I had a sword, ay, the flower of Smithfield for a sword, a right fox, i' faith . . . 't is gone, and there are few good ones made now. I see by this dearth of good swords that dearth of sword-and-buckler fight begins to grow on't; I am sorry for it; I shall never see good manhood again if it be once gone; this poking fight of rapier and dagger will come up then; then a man, a tall man, and a good sword-and-buckler man, will be spitted like a cat or a coney; then a boy will be as good as a man, unless the Lord show mercy unto us; well, I·had as lief be hanged as live to see that day.

If an angry man merely wanted to settle a sudden quarrel with a good gory hand-to-hand, but not carry it to the length of killing, he was ill advised to use a rapier. Giacomo di Grassi, in his *True Arte of Defence* (Englished 1594), well observes that 'the Rapier is generally allowed as a weapon because most perilous, therefore most feared, and thereupon private quarrels and common frayes soonest shunned.'

Can we trace in Day's subsequent writings any reflection of that fatal fight with Porter? It may not be the mere accident of popular demand that in the autumn after he had put a bloody period to the life of a dramatist—one of 'the best for Comedy amongst us'—we find him collaborating with Haughton in writing two tragedies which deal with recent murders: *The Tragedy of Cox of Collumpton* and *Thomas Merry, or Beech's Tragedy*. It was not until the following spring that he made an effort towards comedy in some of the scenes of *The Blind Beggar*. Yet here, if we give a loose to our imaginations under the stimulus of the grim fact just disclosed to us, we may fancy some echo of that tragedy acted to the life in the June of 1599:

> (*Enter Captain Westford and Officers*)
> *Cap. W.* Lay hold on him; and, Mr. Strowd, once more
> Confesse thy guilt.
>   *Old Strowd.* Why, Sir, I not deny
> Sir Robert Westford, doing me much wrong,
> Is by me slain.
>   *Cap. W.* And you for this offence
> Shall be conducted safely unto Prison
> Till matters may be better thought upon:
> Mean time your own confession is my warrant.
>   *O. Str.* Well, Gentlemen, I do obey the Law,
> And will yield my body Prisoner to the King.
> Son, work what means ye can for my repreiue
> Till we may sue for pardon. So adue my Son;
> Heaven give thee grace such desprate bralls to shun.

And, finally, think of Day, a few months after he had slain Porter with his rapier, penning the lines in Act V, where Captain Westford and Young Playnsey, demanding trial by combat before the King, are making choice of weapons:

> *Y. Playn.* Come, Captain Westford, you have been in Spain,
> And are well practis'd in the desperate fight
> Of Single Rapier.
>   *Cap. W.*   Playnsey, I am pleas'd.
>   *King.* So are not we.
> The single Rapier is too desperate;
> And therefore choose some other weapon,
> Or we will have no Combat fought this day.

APPENDICES

SHAKESPEARE'S ASSOCIATES IN THE GATE-HOUSE PURCHASE

SOMETHING OF John Jackson's earlier years and associations is to be learned by following another clue presented by Shakespeare's deed. In the lower right-hand corner of the parchment we read *Recognit' coram me Gre: Donhault: in Cancellar' Magro* ('acknowledged before me Gre: Donhault, Master in Chancery').

We should perhaps make a mistake to pass off this certificate as a dusty formality. For Gregory Donhault (or Downhale) has already been brought to life for us in *Mount Tabor* (1639), the charming autobiography of R. Willis, who was Shakespeare's contemporary, born 1564.[1] Willis relates how Master Gregory Downhale 'of Pembroke Hall in Cambridge' came to be his schoolmaster at Christ's School, Gloucester; how he took a liking to the boy, and with gentleness and familiarity made him love his book. 'He came thither but bachelor of arts, a good scholar, and who wrote both the secretary and the Italian hands exquisitely well. But after a few years that he had proceeded master of arts, finding the school's entertainment not worthy of him, he left it, and betook himself to another course of being secretary to some nobleman, and at last became secretary to the worthy Lord Chancellor Ellesmere, and in that service (as I think)

---

[1] See John Dover Wilson, *Life in Shakespeare's England* (1911 etc.), 52–53.

died.' Willis goes on to say that Downhale's extraordinary help and example were such as to equip his pupil to follow in his footsteps, and to become himself—without benefit of a university education—secretary to Lord Keeper Coventry.

This attractive picture of the rise of a schoolmaster who was both kind and able stirred me to search out his will (P.C.C. 29 Lawe). The testator appears as 'Gregorie Donhaulte, Esquire, now secretary to Lord Ellesmere Lord Chancellor of England,' and the will was made on April 1, 1614, just before his death. Among several points of interest which it presents, the following stand out for our present purpose:

Donhault lived in St. Mary Aldermanbury, the parish of Heminges and Condell.

He left £100 for poor scholars in Cambridge, and another £100 to found a scholarship at Pembroke College.

He mentions 'a diamond ring given the testator by the Countess of Pembroke.' Since no other noble family is named in the will, and since Donhault's attachment to Pembroke College was close, it is more than tempting to conclude from the countess's gift of a diamond ring that the nobleman whom (according to Willis) Donhault served was Henry Earl of Pembroke. Perhaps we may picture Donhault domesticated at Wilton, where 'Sidney's sister, Pembroke's mother' kept court for poets.

And finally we read in Donhault's will of a legacy of £100 (increased by a codicil to £200) to John Jackson, 'who did performe faithfull and true and lovinge service to mee for the space of sundrie yeares.' This is a large bequest, and its terms show personal attachment. If

Jackson's service to Donhault fell in the Pembroke years, his acquaintance with poets was of long standing, and his friendship with Shakespeare and his membership in the Mermaid club seem natural.

We can understand now why the deed was taken to Master Gregory Donhault to be certified. He was a fellow-parishioner of Heminges, and a good friend and former master of Jackson. If he had served in the household of the Countess of Pembroke, he was obviously the man to validate the deed of a great poet!

To continue with our findings about John Jackson, we note that from January 1616 comes an amusing deposition of his in a Chancery suit with a goldsmith over the disputed purchase of a diamond ring two years earlier (C24/426, *Hanbury v. Harrys*). Jackson testifies that 'about two yeares agone the pl*aintiff* [John Hanbury] being accompanyed with this depon*ent* did repayre to the shopp of the def*endant* Harris scytuate in Cheapesyde London to buy a dyamond Ringe' which in the absence of the master was shown them by John Samuell, and for which he asked fifty pounds. Hanbury took the ring away to see if it were suitable, but did not promise to buy it. Afterwards, while Hanbury was in the country, Harrys asked for payment, and Jackson gave him £30. Then Hanbury tried to return the ring to Harrys and have the money refunded. Harrys, however, would give £30 worth of plate but no cash.

Evidently the ready money to which Harrys clung was Jackson's. Having married Jacob James's widow, who was said to have brought him the best part of an estate of £8000 (though £3000 of it was earmarked for the marriage portions of the three James daughters), and being a sharer in the lucrative farm of the duty on sweet wines, Jackson was very well off. In 1615 he shows both his substance and his connection with Yorkshire by standing surety for the composition for first fruits by a minister, Henry Cowper, presented to the rectory of Rise, a few miles north-east of Hull (E334/32). From these years, moreover, we have several bonds or recognizances of debt, and in each case John Jackson is the recognizee or creditor. I list the dates, names, and sums involved: 1613, 17 Dec., Richard Seaman of St. Clement Danes, Midds., gentleman, £200; 1617, 18 Nov., George White of Markby, Lincs., gentleman, £1000; 1618, 2 July, Thomas Trippe of Barton-on-Humber, Lincs., gentleman, John Dighton of Manton, Lincs., gentleman, and Joseph Humphrey of Kingston-upon-Hull, merchant, £40; 1621, 10 May, Abraham Pooke (of St. Andrew by the Wardrobe, London), haberdasher, £1200 (L.C.4/ 198/33^v, 443^v; 199/42, 278^v). Abraham Pooke, the last named, had in 1613 been appointed by Jackson's friend Jacob James his testamentary overseer.

In 1618, two years after Shakespeare's death, Jackson is described as 'esquire' in a brief deposition in Chancery (C24/449, *Cotes v. Cotes*); and in the same year he and the other Shakespeare trustees, John Heminges and William Johnson of the Mermaid, made over the Blackfriars Gate-House to two other trustees, John Greene of Clement's Inn and Mathew Morris of Stratford. This step was taken to carry out the terms of Shakespeare's will, by which Susanna Hall was to have the property (Halliwell-Phillipps, *Outlines* II. 36–41). Mathew Morris, gentleman, had been a trusted servant in Acton of John Hall's father, and had drawn up his will.

Marie James, Jackson's eldest stepdaughter, married a gentleman of Wing, Bucks, called Thomas Jackman; and the £2000 which the latter acknowledged he owed Jackson on July 11, 1623, may have had to do with the marriage settlement (L.C.4/199/483). As already noted, John Jackson made his own will January 26, 1624/5, appointing his wife Jane executrix and residuary legatee, and Thomas Jackman witnessed it. Jackson must have died before April 12, 1625, when the will was proved, and was no doubt buried according to his wish in St. Andrew's Church, across the way from Shakespeare's Blackfriars Gate-House. As a third husband his widow Jane married Richard Crane, esquire. They lived in Buckinghamshire, not many miles from Wing, at Leckhampstead. Our knowledge of this marriage comes from Thomas Jackman's will, dated February 13, 1629/30 (P.C.C. 101 Scroope).

These few certainties about the identity, activities, and surroundings of Shakespeare's two unknown friends Thomas Savage and John Jackson are but a beginning. Large additions may be expected from further exploration.

.   .   .   .   .

We have documents produced at two scenes in Shakespeare's life when he was in the centre of the picture. Concerning one of them, the drawing and executing of his will, much has been written. About the other, his purchase of the Blackfriars Gate-House, we find very little, chiefly for lack of information concerning the persons involved. Let us run over briefly what is known.

There is first the conveyance, dated March 10, 1613, by which Henry Walker, 'citizen and minstrel of London,' for £140 sells to William Shakespeare 'of Stratford upon

Avon in the county of Warwick, gentleman,' William Johnson 'citizen and vintner of London,' John Jackson and John Hemmyngs 'of London, gentlemen,' the Black-friars Gate-House and its plot of ground, with certain reservations, the terms of which show that Shakespeare was the real purchaser and the others his trustees. Evidently Shakespeare paid down only £80 of the purchase money, since there is also a mortgage, dated the following day, March 11, between the same parties, by which Shakespeare and his trustees grant a 100-year lease of the property to Walker at an annual rent of a peppercorn, unless Shakespeare on the September 29 following pay £60 to Walker at his house in St. Martin Ludgate, London.

Both instruments lack Heminges's signature; he was evidently not present. And in both the four witnesses signatory are the same: 'Will: Atkinson, Edw: Ouery, Robert Andrewes, Scr[ivener], Henry Lawrence servant to the same Scr[ivener].' On March 11 the conveyance was acknowledged before a Master in Chancery, Gregory Donhault, for it bears the holograph certificate 'Recognit' coram me Gre: Donhault: in Cancellar' Magro, vndecimo die Martij Anno Supradict'.' The fact that Heminges was absent and the four witnesses the same for both deeds makes one suspect that both were executed at one sitting, March 11, a Thursday in the third week of Lent.

Here are a number of bare and unknown names. Let us see what can be done to lift out of lifelessness this group of men brought together for 'sealing,' in accordance with custom, no doubt at a tavern. Since William Johnson was a party, in all likelihood these instruments were executed at his Mermaid Tavern in Bread Street, a favourite place for such meetings. Of mine host Johnson, and of John Jackson, we already have formed some idea. What of the others?

First, the scriveners who prepared the legal instruments, Robert Andrewes and his servant Henry Lawrence. Andrewes kept his shop in the parish of St. Gregory adjoining St. Paul's. This is in the neighbourhood both of the property being transferred and of the dwelling of Henry Walker the vendor in St. Martin Ludgate. In 1603 Andrewes had drawn the will of Marie the mother of Elias James, for whom Shakespeare wrote an epitaph in 1610. Three years after the date of the deed he drew for Shakespeare, Andrewes died (P.C.C. 78 Cope). Possibly his servant Henry Lawrence, who set up in business for himself, succeeded to the shop in St. Gregory's, since we find him in 1620 witnessing the will of his friend Joel Browne, a barber-surgeon of that parish (P.C.C. 35 Soame).

The witness 'Will: Atkinson' proves from his autograph to be William Atkinson of St. Mary Aldermanbury, gentleman, aged about forty-two, who since 1597 has been Clerk of the Brewers' Company. Stow describes the Brewers' Hall in Addle Street, St. Mary Aldermanbury, as 'a fayre house.' It was set back from the street, in one of whose 'fayre buildings' Heminges lived. As Clerk of the Company, William Atkinson must have known the whole family of Jameses, the brewers of Puddle Wharf—Dericke, Abraham, Marie, Elias, and Jacob—all by this time deceased except Jacob. And as a parishioner of St. Mary's, he was well acquainted with his neighbours John Heminges and William Leveson (Shakespeare's trustees), with Henry Condell, and with Sir John Swinnerton, from whom Jackson was soon to lease part of the farm of sweet wines.

Gregory Donhault (Downhale, Downhall, Downall), the Master in Chancery who certified the acknowledgment of the deed, was another fellow-parishioner of St. Mary Aldermanbury, and possibly made one of the group present at the sealing. This gentleman had formerly, like John Donne, been secretary to Sir Thomas Egerton, the Lord Chancellor. His death in the following year was reported by John Chamberlain to Sir Dudley Carleton, the Ambassador at Venice: 'and Downall [is dead,] somtime the Lord Chauncellors secretarie and now a master of the chauncerie' [17 April 1614, S.P.14/77/6].

The remaining witness, Edward Overy, gentleman, turns out to be closely connected with both sides in the transaction—not only with the vendor Henry Walker, but also with Shakespeare's friend John Jackson. The son of a tanner, Edward Overy had been apprenticed to William Hickes, a wealthy scrivener and merchant of St. Martin Ludgate, and continued to live with him as servant or partner after he was free from his indentures. So greatly did he prosper in business that after his death in 1621, his 'large estate both of lands, leases, goods, and debts to him owing' was the subject of much litigation. By his will (P.C.C. 33 Dale), in which he names his master William Hickes executor and residuary legatee, he bequeaths to his 'kind friend Mr John Jackson' £5, and a ring for his wife. He also remembers his cousin Robert Gill, who had been Henry Walker's apprentice.

Overy's master William Hickes died in the following year, 1622 (P.C.C. 82 Savile), leaving a great estate, part of which is mentioned as his 'stock and adventure in the East India Company' and 'land and adventure in Virginia.' His son Samuel Hickes and his cousin Robert Gill had both been Walker's apprentices. His 'loving friend M[r] John Jackson' is remembered with a ring. Both Overy and Hickes left rings to 'M[r] Pye'—Edmond Pye, attorney of the King's Bench, who at this time was employed in several actions in that court by William Johnson of the Mermaid.

As for the vendor, Henry Walker,[1] he was born at Kington, Herefordshire, on the border of Wales; a member of the Minstrels' or Musicians' Company of London; lived in a house in St. Martin Ludgate belonging to William Hickes, and took Hickes's son Samuel as one of his apprentices. That he was a man of considerable property appears by his will, proved August 30, 1616 (P.C.C. 94 Cope). Both Hickes and Overy witnessed it, and Overy is named an overseer. Among other bequests Walker leaves £120 to the Master, Wardens, and Assistants of the Company of Musicians; they are to allow £8 of the income annually to the churchwardens of his native Kington, to be distributed in bread every Sunday to twenty of the poorest people there.

Would it were possible to apply the White Knight's summary methods to Walker, to oblige him to tell us how he lived, and what it was he did! Presumably he was, or had been, proficient in music, since he was free of the Company of Musicians, and took several apprentices, among them the son of his wealthy landlord. But did

---

[1] A comparison of signatures shows that he is to be distinguished from another Henry Walker, a singing man or petty canon of H.M. Chapel at Windsor (Sta. Cha. 5/F21/21, F24/33; C3/230/69).

he gain his wealth by playing at weddings or under windows or in taverns? It has been asserted that the Musicians' Company was the only city livery company for the exercise of a profession (actors were notoriously not so privileged); and the charter granted by King James in 1604 gave it control over the public performance of music.

Though Walker was no doubt a proficient performer, I find that he was also a shopkeeper at his house in St. Martin Ludgate; but the nature of his wares remains annoyingly unspecified. On Friday, May 1, 1607, a holiday, he opened his shop for business, and his neighbours the churchwardens presented him for it to the Bishop's official (Lib. Act. in Negoc. Offic. Lond., 1607–1608, f. 74, February 15, 1607/8): 'Walker, Henry, of St. Martin Ludgate. xij^d Presented for opening his shopp and hanging out wares uppon Maye daye last Comparuit &c to acknowledge his fault in Church on Sunday next and certify' (Ibid., April 5, 1608) 'Walker, Henry, St. Martin Ludgate. To certify of his publique acknowledging his fault in the churche for opening his shopp & hanging forthe wares on Maye daye last. Comparuit &c.' Did these wares have to do with music? Possibly not; examples of freemen of London exercising a trade different from that of the company to which they belonged are frequent. Yet possibly Walker sold musical instruments, which presumably would be in request on May Day!

To return for a final glance at the scene of Shakespeare's purchase in 1613, conjured up from the evidence of the engrossed, signed, sealed, witnessed, and certified deeds. From what we have learned by following the clues presented, we can see that it was unquestionably an har-

monious group that assembled, probably at the Mermaid
Tavern, for the sealing between the minstrel and the ex-
player and dramatist. Mine host Johnson makes them
welcome with his best wine. Mr. Atkinson, Clerk of the
Brewers' Company, is well known to Mr. Jackson and to
frequenters of St. Mary Aldermanbury. The Master in
Chancery, Mr. Donhault, is a neighbour of Atkinson's,
and of Mr. Shakespeare's friends, Heminges and Condell.
Mr. Overy is a close friend both of Mr. Walker and of Mr.
Jackson. It would be pleasant if we could preserve this
genial scene like a fly in amber, and not look ahead three
years. Before the end of 1616 the scrivener, the Master in
Chancery, and the principals—Walker and Shakespeare—
had all disappeared.

SHAKESPEARE RECORDS

1. A HOLINSHED LINK

W AS JOHN SHAKESPEARE, the father of William, the
first Shakespeare to live in Stratford-on-Avon?
Everyone knows that in the first chapter of his monu-
mental study of Shakespeare, Sir Edmund Chambers, the
most cautious and reliable of the poet's biographers,
has the following passage: 'His father, John Shakespeare,
was not of native Stratford stock; there are no Shakespeares in the gild register. John makes his first appearance in Stratford at a leet of 29 April, 1552, when he was
fined one shilling for having an unauthorized dunghill in
Henley St.' All Shakespeare biographers, indeed, apparently believe that the poet's father was the first of the
Warwickshire Shakespeares (who were plentiful in the
country north of Stratford) to find his way to the town.
Recent research is at hand to shake this belief. Thanks
to the assistance of my friend Mr. J. H. Morrison, I can
announce the discovery of two hitherto unknown John
Shakespeares of Stratford.

The first of these is a certain 'John Shakespeare of
Stratford upon Avon, yeoman,' under the date of Easter,
1533. The date 1533—nineteen years before the first
mention of Shakespeare's father, and twenty-three or
twenty-four years before the marriage with Mary Arden,
makes it extremely improbable that this new John Shakespeare of Stratford, already in 1533 grown to manhood

and in business, can be identified with Shakespeare's father, or with John Shakespeare of Ingon, or with John Shakespeare of Clifford Chambers, or with the corvizer John Shakespeare found in Stratford between 1586 and 1595. It seems clear, then, that we are here confronted with another John Shakespeare of Stratford. In the present state of our knowledge we cannot be certain what, if any, was the relation of this earlier John of Stratford to the poet's father. But since Sir Edmund Chambers, after a critical examination of all the evidence, admits that we are not sure that Richard Shakespeare of Snitterfield was the poet's grandfather, it is evident that we must push our researches further before we can be satisfied that we know even the second step in the pedigree of the greatest English man of letters.

The second clue relates not only to another new John Shakespeare but to Raphael Holinshed. It is hardly necessary to repeat that it was Shakespeare's use of Holinshed's compilation that has made the chronicler's name a household word. Of all Shakespeare's books Holinshed's *Chronicles* was easily of the greatest service to him. From it he obtained not only the substance and some-times the very language of his English historical plays, but his knowledge of the ancient heroic tales of King Lear, Macbeth, and Cymbeline. Sir Walter Raleigh considered Shakespeare fortunate in that the 'Chronicles of Holin-shed, unlike more modern histories, are dramatic in essence; they leave constitutional problems on one side and make the most of striking events and characters.' Holinshed's work was deservedly successful, gaining an immediate and wide popularity.

When we turn from Holinshed's work to the chronicler himself, we might if we chose make as great a mystery out of his life as some writers have made of Shakespeare's, since a good deal less is known of its external facts. W. G. Boswell-Stone, the editor of *Shakespeare's Holinshed*, confesses that of his author 'we know nothing save what his will reveals.' Sir Sidney Lee, who contributed a sketch of Holinshed to the *Dictionary of National Biography*, writes:

> He made his will on 1 October, 1578, and there describes himself as steward to Thomas Burdet of Bramcote, Warwickshire. Wood says that he died at Bramcote about the end of 1580. By his will, which was proved on 24 April, 1582, all his property passed to his master, Burdet, who thus, according to Wood, became possessor of Holinshed's "notes, collections, books, and MSS." The only manuscript of Holinshed known to be extant is a translation prepared for the "Chronicle" of Florence of Worcester, which is now in Brit. Mus. MS. Harl. 563.

This account is inaccurate in three particulars. In the first place, Holinshed in his will does not describe himself as steward to Thomas Burdett. Though in fact he was Burdett's steward, in the will he merely calls Burdett his master. In the second place, his will was proved not on April 24, 1582, but on April 24, 1581. And in the third place, the manuscript translation of Florence of Worcester in Manuscript Harley 563 has been shown to be not in Holinshed's hand, but in that of John Stow.

The fact that the will was proved not in the spring of 1582 but in that of 1581 makes it more likely that Wood is correct in fixing the date of Holinshed's death about the end of 1580. I have looked up the registered copy of

Holinshed's will at the Principal Probate Registry,
Somerset House [14 Darcy]. It runs as follows:

> In the name of God, Amen. I Raphaell Hollinshed
> of Bromcote in the Countie of Warr', ordaine and make
> my laste will and testamente, in manner and forme
> followinge,. Firste I bequeathe my synnefull sowle to
> allmightie god, the creator of me and all mankinde,
> trusting that by the merrittes and bloudsheddinge of
> his deere sonne Jesus christe he will pardonne me of all
> mine offences, and place my saide sinnefull sowle,
> washed and pourged from the filthe of synne, amounge
> the number of his electe in the blesse of heauen.
> Secoundlie for my worldlie goodes whatsoever the
> same bee, wherein I haue anye propertie to geve and
> bestowe the same I geue and bequeathe theme and
> everie parte and percell of theme vnto my maister
> Thomas Burdette of Bromecotte aforesaide esquire
> makinge and constitutinge him my onelie and sole exe-
> cutoure. In witnes whereof I haue writtenne this my
> laste will and testamente with mine owne hande and
> subscribed my name and putte to my seale the firste daie
> of October in the yeare of oure lorde god a thowsande
> fyve hundred seaventie and eighte per me Raphaelem
> Hollingshed. [Proved at London 24 April 1581 by the
> oath of Peter Johnson notary public, 'procuratoris
> Thome Burdette executoris.']

Since Holinshed's testament reads, 'I haue writtenne
this my laste will and testamente with mine owne hande
and subscribed my name,' I thought that a search for
the original will at Somerset House might yield result.
But Mr. Pettit, superintendent of the Department for
Literary Inquiry, who kindly undertook the search, reported that it cannot be found. I then turned to the legal
archives in the Public Record Office, and here I was
more fortunate. I found not only a sworn answer of

Holinshed to a bill of complaint in Chancery, but an original signature of the chronicler to the engrossed document: 'By me Raphaell Holenshed.'

The importance of this Chancery suit, however, is not that it contains an autograph of Holinshed, but what is revealed about his activities. It will be remembered that Holinshed lived with his master, Thomas Burdett, esquire, at Bramcote in Warwickshire, some distance north and east of Stratford. But this suit reveals that Burdett was lord of the Manor of Packwood, situated in and about the small village of Packwood, a place much closer to Shakespeare's town; it also reveals that Raphael Holinshed, as Burdett's steward, used for many years to come regularly to Packwood to preside over the manor court, grant copyhold leases, and look after his master's interests. As he himself says in his Chancery answer, he was 'of Long time Steward vnto the said Thomas Burdett of the said Manor [of Packwood], and by his commandement kept diverse and sundrie Courtes there and made many Coppies accordinge to the Custome of the said Manor of sundrie seuerall messuages, Landes, and tenementes within the same Manor.'

Holinshed was there at least as early as 1561, three years before Shakespeare's birth, and continued his intimate acquaintance with the affairs of Packwood until his death at the close of 1580, less than two years before William Shakespeare married Anne Hathaway. I wish to suggest, therefore, that in point of time and proximity Shakespeare as a youth might very well have been acquainted with Holinshed during the period when the chronicles were being compiled. What makes this hypothesis more attractive is a hitherto unsuspected connection between Pack-

wood and Stratford. It has long been known that in the
first half of the sixteenth century a family of Shakespeares
lived in the village of Packwood. The father of the family,
Christopher Shakespeare, died about 1551. One of his
daughters had married William Featherstone, a member
of the leading family of the village, whose fine old four-
teenth-century mansion, Packwood House, is still standing, surrounded by beautiful gardens and groves of oak,
one of the show places of Shakespeare's country. Christopher Shakespeare's sons, William, Richard, Roger,
Christopher, and John, survived him. All of these must
have been familiarly known to Raphael Holinshed, the
steward of the manor of Packwood.

I have now found proof in a lawsuit of 1561,[1] which
names three of these Shakespeare brothers, that John
Shakespeare (possibly the youngest of the sons) had
moved to Stratford-on-Avon. The description runs as
follows: 'Richard Shackspere of Packwood,' 'John
Shackspere of Stretford Apon Aven,' and 'Roger Shackspere of Pacwood.' John Shakespeare of Packwood was
therefore living in Stratford three years before the birth
of William Shakespeare, the future poet, to John and
Mary Shakespeare. Here then is a connection between
the Shakespeares of Packwood, where Holinshed, the
chronicler, was steward of the manor, and a Shakespeare
of Stratford.

I am not rash enough to claim that William Shakespeare's propensity, when he was seeking material for a
play, to turn to the four heavy folios put together by his
learned neighbour Holinshed proves that they were on
terms of intimate friendship. But for the possibility of such

---

[1] C.P. 40/1190/211.

a friendship there now seems something to be said; and I hope that future research will supply us with more.

2. JOHN SHAKESPEARE'S QUARREL

It is gratifying to find that even in these later days we have not yet come to the end of Shakespearean disclosures. A fortunate discovery among the documents of the Public Record Office enables me to throw some light on the doings of John Shakespeare in 1582. In this year his eighteen-year-old son William married Anne Hathaway.

As part of an exhaustive search through the Controlment Rolls of the Court of Queen's (King's) Bench for the reigns of Elizabeth and James I, I examined the lists of entries of 'petitions for sureties of the peace.' In quarrels in which blows were perhaps given and threats of physical violence certainly uttered, if the offended party could take his oath in Court that he was in actual fear of violence or death, the Court would have before it the party complained of, and bind him over to keep the peace: that is, oblige him and (usually) two sureties to enter sufficient bond against a breach.

All manner of quarrels and hot words must lie behind these brief entries on the Controlment Rolls. With that thought in mind, it was exciting to come, in the long file of petitioners, on the name of John Shakespeare. Abbreviations expanded, the record of the Shakespeare case is as follows:

> Anglia scire scilicet Johannes Shakespere petit securitates pacis versus Radulphum Cawdrey, Willelmum Russell, Thomam Logginge, & Robertum Young, ob metum mortis & mutulacione membrorum suorum.

Attachiamentum vicecomiti Warr' retornabile octa-
bis Michaelis. [K.B. 29/217.]

This entry, made in Trinity term (June 15–July 4), 1582,
may be translated thus:

England Be it known that John Shakespere craves
sureties of the peace against Ralph Cawdrey, William
Russell, Thomas Logginge, and Robert Young, for
fear of death and mutilation of his limbs.

Writ of attachment to the sheriff of Warwickshire,
returnable on the octave of St. Michael [October 6,
1582].

The phrase 'for fear of death and mutilation of his limbs'
is the common form, appearing in all these entries of
petitions for sureties of the peace.

We are able to clear away at once any suspicion that
this John Shakespeare may be the corvizer, or shoemaker,
and not the father of the poet: for at this date the shoemaker was still living in the town of Warwick, and it will
be seen from what follows that this is a Stratford quarrel.
Our first concern is to identify these men, who, as John
Shakespeare swore, had threatened him with personal
violence or death. Publication of the Corporation Records of Stratford has familiarized us with many of
Shakespeare's fellow-townsmen, and the names of Ralph
Cawdrey and Robert Young spring immediately to the
eye. Ralph Cawdrey was a dominant personage in
Stratford. He served one of his terms as High Bailiff of
the borough in 1568, and was succeeded in office the
following year by John Shakespeare. To describe him
further, let me quote a paragraph from Mr. Fripp's interesting book *Shakespeare's Stratford*:

Bridge Street: At the 'Chure' in Middle Row were the 'Shambles' and the shop (or rather shops) of Alderman Rafe Cawdrey, a butcher and a Catholic, whose wife and daughters were recusants and his son a fugitive Jesuit priest. He was tenant under the Corporation of the fourth inn of the town, an ancient hostel, the property of the Gild, rebuilt by them in 1467–9, the Angel at the top of Back Bridge Street on the right, adjoining Henley Street.

Cawdrey's son George, later the recusant, is the subject of an amusing entry in the Corporation minutes for January 15, 1577–8, when he was a boy of 12:

> Record this
> George Cawdrie the sonne of Raffe Cawdrie at his age of iiij yeres had his left yere [*i.e.*, ear] disfigured wth [a] horse.

The father was evidently anxious to get the accident on record, so that the lopsided appearance of his son's head might not later be construed by evil-minded persons as the result of a collision with the law.

In the light of Alderman Shakespeare's quarrel with Alderman Cawdrey in 1582, the relations of the two in the years preceding take on a new interest; and it will be seen that there is no evidence that the two were ever on friendly terms. First we find Shakespeare in 1557 becoming a mainpernor, or surety, for William Wyngfyld, when Cawdrey was suing the latter for debt. In the year following Shakespeare was sworn in as one of the four constables of Stratford; and he was still doing constabulary duty in the spring of 1559, when Cawdrey was fined for making a fray upon Alexander Webbe of Bearley, who was the brother-in-law of Constable Shakespeare's wife, Mary (Arden) Shakespeare. Let us hope that Shakespeare had the satisfaction of stopping the fight, rescuing his relative, and arresting the bellicose butcher, Cawdrey.

A few months later a legal action between John Shakespeare and Richard Court was referred to Cawdrey and John Ichiver for determination or report. Although thus appointed to act coolly as a referee or judge, Cawdrey was still of a turbulent spirit. The following entry, under date of October 5, 1560, is marked *nota bene*: 'Raff Cawdrey for makynge afray vppon . . . grene of wotton he stands amerced.' Cawdrey was well-to-do. These fines cannot have troubled him greatly. It may be recalled that 1564, the year of the poet Shakespeare's birth, was a year of severe plague; and in a list of contributions for the relief of sufferers we find: 'M^r. Cavdre ij^s' and 'Jhon shacksper xij^d.'

Everybody knows that in 1577 Alderman Shakespeare suddenly left off attending the meetings or 'halls' of the corporation, and that, with the exception of perhaps two occasions, he never attended again. What was the cause of his withdrawal? Pecuniary embarrassment has been doubtfully advanced as an explanation. Our new document, with its disclosure of a violent quarrel in 1582, points to the more likely reason that Shakespeare was at odds with some of the most influential townsmen. This surmise is confirmed when we realize that in 1582, when Shakespeare swore the peace against Cawdrey, the latter was once more in office as High Bailiff of Stratford. We are still ignorant of the origins of the ill-feeling. But, whatever they may have been, we know that irritation had mounted to such a pitch by the late spring of 1582 that John Shakespeare was able to take his corporal oath that four men had threatened him with physical violence, one of whom was the executive head of the borough of Stratford.

Such strife and bickering provided no very peaceful atmosphere for the rural springtime love-making of young Shakespeare and Anne Hathaway. But we may suppose that when parents meditate neighbourly violence and bandy threats with their enemies, sweet lovers love the spring all the more, and find their refuge in it. Anne Hathaway was not a Cawdrey, and no parallel with Montagues and Capulets can be drawn.

The elder Shakespeare's enemies, as we have seen, included three others besides Alderman Cawdrey: William Russell, Thomas Logginge, and Robert Young. The last named was a well-known dyer of Stratford, who four years after the quarrel married Margery, a sister of Shakespeare's friend, Richard Field. Young died early in 1595. In the autumn following, his widow Margery was involved in a law-suit with Widow Joan Perrott. Widow Young insisted that some goods, sold on August 25 by Widow Perrott, had been 'deceitfully' appropriated from her. Among them were three Prayer-books, valued at 10s. bought by Master Barber of the Bear, and 'one book,' not valued, purchased by 'Master Shakespeare.' This Master Shakespeare may be John, the old alderman; in which case (if he bought the book to read) we have evidence not only that he could read, but also that he valued reading. But 'Master Shakespeare' may more probably be the son, William, in which case we may deplore the omission of the title of the book.

It is difficult to throw much light on William Russell and Thomas Logginge. A William Russell appears in the Stratford parish registers as the father of four children christened between 1571 and 1575. This William Russell is no doubt Shakespeare's enemy of 1582. As for Thomas Logginge, the difficulties of identification are greater. I find a Thomas Loggyn, a haberdasher of London, whose will was proved in 1609. Also there was a family of Loggins at Swalcliff, Oxfordshire, which had relations with Stratford in the beginning and middle of the seventeenth century, but I have not traced a Thomas of earlier date.

It is reasonable to think of John Shakespeare's declining years as more peaceful than those which had gone before. By 1596 his son William was well established in success, and the remaining five years of the elder man's life must have been free from pecuniary cares. He had at least the satisfaction of outliving his antagonists, Cawdrey and Young, who died in 1588 and 1595 respectively.

3. THREE SHAKESPEARES

Of the following discoveries of Shakespearean interest, the first presents a William Shakespere, hitherto unnoticed, of Mansfield, Nottinghamshire, son of Robert and Elizabeth Shakespere, and grandson of Richard Shakespere. He describes himself in a Chancery bill of November 18, 1561, as 'a contynuall dweller in the Citie of London.' (Public Record Office, C3/166/85.)

The next relates to the litigation discovered by Halliwell-Phillipps, and rediscovered by Mrs. Stopes (Coram Rege Roll 1361, mem. 293). In 1600 a William Shackspere recovered by suit in the Court of Queen's Bench a debt of £7 from John Clayton, yeoman, of Willington, Bedfordshire. The debt had been acknowledged May 22, 1592. Of this William Shackspere Sir Sidney Lee writes, 'There is nothing to identify John Clayton's creditor with the dramatist, nor is it easy to explain why he should have lent money to a Bedfordshire yeoman.' Sir Edmund Chambers agrees with Lee that there is no ground for identifying this Shackspere with the dramatist. Mrs. Stopes, on the other hand, inclined to an identification.

I think I have found a William Shakespeare who meets the requirements of the case and removes any difficulty. Acting on the assumption that Clayton's creditor would be likely to be an inhabitant of Bedfordshire, I searched the subsidy rolls for that county. In the roll for 1593 (E179/72/213) I found John Cleyton, a husbandman of Willington, and on casting about, in a roll for 1596 (E179/243/2) I turned up William Shakespeare, husbandman, of Campton, Bedfordshire. Campton is some eight miles south of Willington. With this new light, I think we may regard the question as settled.

The next item relates to Gilbert, a younger brother of the dramatist. Halliwell-Phillipps said he had discovered Gilbert Shakespeare described as a London haberdasher, standing as one of the sureties for a Stratford 'clock-maker.' He gave no reference, and Mrs. Stopes was unable to trace the entry. But she searched the books of the Haberdashers' Company, and, finding no Gilbert Shakespeare, but noting a Gilbert Shepheard, she suggested that Halliwell-Phillipps had made a mistake, and had read Shakespeare for Shepheard. I have run the entry down (K.B.27/1345, Trin. 39 Eliz.) and vindicated Halliwell-Phillipps on the point, except that he read *clookmaker* (that is, cloakmaker) as *clockmaker*. The principal is William Sampson 'de Stratford super Aven in Comitatu Warr', Clookmaker,' and his two pledges are Richard Johnson 'de parochia sancte Brigitte, London', Shomaker,' and Gilbert Shackspere 'de parochia sancte Brigitte predicte, haberdasher.' Although the books of the Haberdashers' Company may fail to mention him, I am confident that we are dealing here with the brother of the dramatist.

I have reserved the most important discovery for the last. It is a new record of the dramatist's father, John Shakespeare, and throws an interesting light on the son's early days in Stratford. A tradition firmly established at Stratford, which, however, cannot be traced farther back than Betterton's visit, describes John Shakespeare as a wool-dealer. Following are the relevant passages taken from Sir Edmund Chambers's invaluable work: Nicholas Rowe (1709): 'His Father, who was a considerable Dealer in Wool . . .' John Jordan (*ca.* 1790): '. . . the father, who it is said was a considerable dealer in wool; for this we have not only the tradition of Stratford, but also the authority of Mr. Rowe.' Sir Richard Phillips (1818): 'The landlord of the Swan and Maidenhead . . . assured the writer, that, when he re-laid the floors of the parlour, the remains of wool, and the refuse of wool-combing, were found under the old flooring, imbedded with the earth of the foundation . . .'

It is to be noted, however, that we have had no documentary proof of the elder Shakespeare's dealings in wool. Such proof is now forthcoming from the following suit in the Court of Common Pleas, brought by John Shakespeare in Trinity Term, 1599, two years before his death:

Warr' ss Johannes Walford nuper de Marlborowe in Comitatu Wiltes' yoman summonitus fuit ad respondendum Johanni Shakespere de placita quod reddat ei viginti & vnam libras quas ei debet & iniuste detinet

&c. Et vnde idem Johannes Shakespere per Willelmum Court Attornatum suum dicit quod cum predictus Johannes Walford quarto die Novembris Anno regni domine Regine nunc decimo apud Stretford super Avon' emisset de eodem Johanne Shakespere viginti & vnam toddas lane vocatum *toddes of wooll* pro predictis viginti & vna libris soluendis eidem Johanni Shakespere cum inde requisitus fuisset; predictus tamen Johannes Walford licet sepius requisitus predictas viginti & vnam libras eidem Johanni Shakes*ρ*ere nondum reddidit sed illas ei hucusque reddere contradixit & adhuc contradicit; vnde dicit quod deterioratus est & dampnum habet ad valenciam decem librarum. Et inde producit sectam &c.

Et predictus Johannes Walford per Stephanum Henchman Attornatum suum venit Et defendit vim & iniuriam quando &c. Et dicit quod ipse non debet prefato Johanni Shakespere predictas viginti & vnam libras nec aliquam denarium inde in forma qua idem Johannes Shakespere superius versus eum narrauit. Et hoc paratus est defendere contra ipsum & sectam suam prout Curia Regine hic constituet; Ideo consideratum est quod predictus Johannes Walford vadetur ei inde legem suam se duodecima manu plegia de lege Johannes Den Ricardus Fen Et veniat cum lege sua hic a die sancti Michaelis in vnum mensem Et dictum est prefato Attornato predicti Johannis Walford quod tunc habeat hic eundem Johannem Walford magistrum suum in propria persona sua ad perficiendum legem suam predictam si &c. (C.P. 40/1626/353d.)

John Shakespeare, by his attorney William Court, sues John Walford, yeoman, of Marlborough, Wiltshire, on a debt of £21; alleging that on November 4, 1568, at Stratford-on-Avon, Walford bought twenty-one tods of wool of him for £21, payable on demand. Walford has never paid, and Shakespeare demands his money, and £10 damages. In reply, Walford, by his attorney Stephen Henchman, denies that he owes Shakespeare anything, and is ready to prove his contention. The Court orders Henchman to have his client Walford in Court on October 29, 1599, for further hearing of the case. Later proceedings are noted in the docket for the following term, but the plea roll containing them has unfortunately been lost. Further light on Walford comes to me by the kindness of Mr. H. C. Brentnall. John Walford served twice as Chamberlain of the borough of Marlborough—1583 and 1586; and three times as its Mayor—1592, 1596, and 1609. I may add that in his will of 1616 (P.C.C. 18 Cope) Walford is described as a clothier.

In John Shakespeare's lawsuit we have evidence of fairly extensive dealing in wool. We are reminded of the mental arithmetic of the Clown in *The Winter's Tale* (4.2):

> Let me see: Every 'leven wether tods; every tod yields pound and odd shilling: fifteen hundred shorn, what comes the wool to?

When the poet was four years old his father sold wool at a pound a tod; the price had risen a trifle by the time of the writing of *The Winter's Tale*. If 'every 'leven wether tods,' the Walford transaction involved the fleeces of 231 Cotswold (or Warwickshire) lions. To the Stratford glover's by-activities in barley and timber we may now confidently add dealings in wool; and perhaps see a basis in fact for Halliwell-Phillipps's designation of the eastern house in Henley-street as the 'Woolshop.'

4. BURBAGE *V.* SHAKESPEARE

When, in a recent search through the docket rolls of the Court of Common Pleas for the latter years of Eliza-

beth's reign, I came upon a suit indexed 'London Bartlett
pro Burbage ffoster pro Shakespeare' in Michaelmas term,
1588, my excitement was natural. Every student of Shakespeare's life has wondered just how it was that he became
acquainted with the Burbages. But to find the Plea Roll
numbered C.P.40/1473, which contained the particulars
of the suit, so decayed as to be 'unfit for production,'
was annoying in the extreme.

I went on in hope, however, through the docket roll
of the next term, Hilary, 1588–9, and was rewarded by
another entry of the same suit. The key-index referred
me to C.P.40/1697, a roll seriously damaged, but still
legible in parts. Membrane 327, on which are enrolled the
particulars of the Burbage–Shakespeare suit, shows a
large rotted spot, covering the greater part of the first
seven lines of the record. On going further into the docket
rolls I turned up an entry of an order in the same suit in
Easter term, 1592—C.P.40/1497, membrane 1122. Neither
of these, to my knowledge, has been published hitherto.

Unfortunately the litigants are not Richard or James
Burbage and William Shakespeare, but an unidentified
William Burbage and the poet's father John. The documents follow. I have tried to indicate the lacunae, and,
with the help of my friend Mr. T. F. T. Plucknett, to extend the numerous abbreviations.

'London' Johannes Shakes ... summonitus fuit ad
respondendum Willelmo Burbage de ... &c. Et unde
idem Willelmus per Thomam ... rto die Julij Anno
domini millesimo quingent ... in Warda de Chepe
posuissent se in arbitr ... arnshurst Willelmi Badger
et Johannis Lytton Arbitratorum ... vnum tenemen-
tum cum pertinentiis in Stratford super Avon' predicta
per prefatum Johannem eidem Willelmo in con[sid-

234

eracionem septem?] librarum et decem solidorum per
eundem Willelmum prefato Johanni in manibus solu-
torum pro diversis annis tunc venturis dimissum vnde
lis et debata inter eos adtunc orte fuissent predictique
Arbitratores accipientes
inter partes predictos
super se onus arbitrandi ʌ de et super premissis predicto
vicesimo quarto die Julij Anno supradicto apud London' in parochia et warda predictis ordinauerunt et arbi-
trati fuerunt quod predictus Johannes relaxaret eidem
Willelmo Burbage bargainam predictam Ac quod predictus Johannes Shackspere solueret eidem Willelmo
septem libras ad festum sancti michaelis archangeli
anno domini millesimo quingentesimo octogesimo
secundo apud signum de le maiden hedd in Stratford
predicta inter horas primam et quartam horologij post
meridiem eiusdem
plus inde in dorso
diei per quod accio accreuit eidem Willelmo ad exi-
gendum et habendum de prefato Johanne predictas
septem libras predictus tamen Johannes licet sepius
requisitus predictas septem libras eidem Willelmo
nondum reddidit set illas ei hucusque reddere contradixit et adhuc contradicit Unde dicit quod deterioratus
est Et dampnum habet ad valenciam decem librarum
Et inde producit sectam &c.
Et predictus Johannes per Willelmum ffoster attornatum suum venit Et defendit vim et iniuriam quando
&c Et dictum est eidem attornato predicti Johannis
quod pro eodem Johanne magistro suo prefato Willelmo in loquela predicta respondeat Et idem attornatus
dicit quod ipse non est informatus per eundem
Johannem magistrum suum de aliquo responso pro
eodem Johanne prefato Willelmo in loquela predicta
dando Et nichil aliud inde dicit per quod idem Willelmus [*rectè* Johannes] remanet versus prefatum Johannem [*rectè* Willelmum] indefensus Ideo consideratum

est quod predictus Willelmus recuperet versus prefatum Johannem debitum suum predictum Et dampna
sua occasione detencionis debiti illius ad triginta et sex
solidos eidem Willelmo ex assensu suo per Curiam hic
adiudicata Et predictus Johannes in misericordia &c.

[C.P.40/1697, mem. 327. Hilary 31 Eliz.]

London' Preceptum fuit vicecomiti Cum Willelmus Burbage nuper in Curia Regine hic scilicet Ter-
mino sancti hillarij anno regni dicte domine Regine
nunc tricesimo primo coram Edmundo Anderson
milite et socijs suis tunc Justiciariis ipsius domine
Regine de Banco hic per Consideracionem eiusdem
Curie recuperasset versus Johannem Shakespeare de
Stratford super Avon' in Comitatu Warr' seniorem
Glover tam quoddam debitum septem librarum quam
triginta et sex solidos quos eidem Willelmo in eadem
Curia hic adiudicatos fuerunt pro dampnis suis que
habuit occasione detencionis debiti illius vnde con-
victus est prout per recordum et processum inde in
eadem Curia hic residentes liquet manifeste execucio
tamen iudicij predicti adhuc restat facienda prout ex
insinuacione predicti Willelmi acceperat Regina Et
quia &c. quod per probos &c scire facias prefato
Johanni quod esset hic ad hunc diem scilicet a die
Pasche in quindecim dies ostencare si quid &c quare
predictus Willelmus execucionem versus prefatum
Johannem de debito et dampnis predictis habere non
debeat iuxta formam recuperacionis predicte si &c Et
modo hic ad hunc diem venit predictus Willelmus per
Rogerum Stackhouse attornatum suum Et predictus
Johannes quarto die placiti solempniter exactus non
venit Et vicecomes modo mandat quod nichil
habet &c nec est inuentus &c Ideo consideratum est
quod predictus Willelmus habeat execucionem versus
prefatum Johannem de debito et dampnis predictis per
ipsius Johannis defaltam &c.

[C.P.40/1497 mem. 1122. Easter 34 Eliz.]

By the first entry, Hilary 1588–9, it appears that John Shakespeare, for an illegible number of pounds (perhaps seven) and ten shillings, had leased to William Burbage a house in Stratford-on-Avon for divers years; and that over this lease lawsuit and contention had arisen between them. To settle the matter they had submitted to the arbitrament of William Badger, John Lytton, and a certain '. . . arnshurst.' These arbitrators determined that Shakespeare should give Burbage's lease back to him, and pay him £7 on Michaelmas Day, 1582, at the sign of the 'Maiden Hedd' in Stratford-on-Avon between 1 and 4 of the clock in the afternoon. On the strength of this award Burbage might bring an action for the £7; but although he frequently demanded his money, John Shakespeare steadily refused and still refuses to pay. Burbage sues for the debt, with £10 damages. Shakespeare makes no defence. Therefore adjudged that Burbage should recover his debt, and 36*s.* damages.

The second entry is an order in Easter Term, 1592, which, after reciting the record of judgment in the foregoing cause between William Burbage and 'John Shakespeare, of Stratford-on-Avon, county Warwick, senior, Glover,' declares that execution of the judgment remains to be done. John Shakespeare is summoned to show cause why William should not have execution against him. Failing to appear after his three days of grace, Shakespeare defaults, and the Court awards the execution against him.

These documents are interesting from more than one point of view. There is first the record of a house in Stratford owned by the poet's father which he had let at some time before 1582. We know already that at this time

Shakespeare owned a house in Greenhill Street purchased in 1556, and the two adjoining Henley Street houses—the eastern (later an inn), purchased in 1556, and the western ('Birthplace'), purchased in 1575.

The names of the arbitrators, to whose award Shakespeare and Burbage submitted, have an interest in themselves. As to the identity of '. . . arnshurst,' I think it is not too hazardous to suggest Nicholas Barnshurst, Shakespeare's old friend and colleague in the Corporation. William Badger is the name of a well-to-do brother of the draper George Badger, Shakespeare's next-door neighbour. Of John Lytton I can find no trace in the Stratford records. A 'John Litton, clerk,' was married in Lapworth in 1593.

But who is this William Burbage, the tenant with whom John Shakespeare's disagreement lasted for so many years? John Burbage, it will be recalled, was bailiff in 1555, and was buried April 3, 1558. But William Burbage's name appears nowhere in the registers of baptisms, marriages, and burials. Who was he, and what was his connection with Shakespeare? It is at least a coincidence that William Burbage had been a tenant of John Shakespeare for some time before the young Shakespeare went up to London and made the acquaintance of James and Richard Burbage.

APPENDIX C

EDICTS OF THE PRINCE DE L'AMOUR

A Coppy of Certayne Edicts made & published by yᵉ commaund of yᵉ right high & mighty Prince, the Prince De L'Amour, to be observed & put in execution by all his loveinge Subjects.

Whereas it hath bin yᵉ custome of the most renowned Princes for wisdome and prudence in all Ages, accordinge as enormities hapened within their Realmes & Dominions, by timely provicion not only to repress them, but also to prevent the like to come. Wee out of our Princely care of yᵉ weale of this our Kingdome of Love, have thought fitt with the advise of our Privy Counsell only, not callinge at the time (the hast of our occasions pressinge vs) our right trusty and wellbeloved the States of our Parliament, to occurr & meet with yᵉ present disorders which wee have observed within this our Realme.

Willing and commaundinge all our Loveing Subjects whome it shall concerne to bee conformable & put in due execucion theese our Edicts following which wee out of our Princely Care, have caused to be published for the good of our Subjects.

AN EDICT AGAINST THE FALCE DYING OF LOVE

Beinge ready at all times to receive yᵉ humble complaincts of all our loveinge Subjects, Wee have found of late many & Sundry bills, of severall persons, who by ill advise have thruste themselves into Conjugall Society representing to vs the great abuse they have suffered by reason of yᵉ alienacion of their wives affeccions from

239

them vnder a pretence of a certaine Platonicke Love (as they call it) y^t vnder that falce Color they may the more secretely convay their Loves from their Husbands pretendinge y^t the person or persons to be loved have a faire & amiable Soule: of which well advising with our Counsell learned in ye Lawes of Love, find this but a subtilty to draw in Plurality of Servants to married Ladyes: for we are not ignorant how incapable the Soule, (beinge an immateriall substance & not subject to view or touch) nor to bee well apparrelled or perfum'd[)] is of any Ladyes Love, nor can wee once imagine y^t any Lady, especially a Court Lady can arrive at y^t height of contemplacion which requires a pacificacion of ye passions, & depression of ye Sences, which when they most endeavor to please or highten wee conceive it impossible that they should grow to any kind of perfection in this Love Wee do therefore, by this Edict, confiscate all such love so falcely Colord and do straitly charge and Commaund the Officers of Chequer to seize & see it deliuerd into our Treasury ther to remaine for the vse of schollers, & such as by great travaile & study haue proceeded to some contemplation of ye soule: & wee doe by these presents peremptorily Forbid any such person or persons from henceforth to vse any such false colours, or to take into their foule [*struck through*] prophane mouths the name of divine Plato, or to make him any way lenocinate to their base desires vnder paine of having their ignorance & adultery discovered both at once.

An Edict against diffidence

Wheras the due state of magnificence of our Royal Court requiring, we haue thought fit to haue about us such servants, as may best doe vs honour as well in their persons & garbe, as in their qualityes & abilityes of mind, & for that we haue observed many of our said servants for want of practising the world, & travailing to forraine parts, to faile of that assurance which as we are informed is used in the Courts of other Princes, & especially in the Court of great Brittaine, we therefore Command that from hence forth every soul of our Servants shall arme their Countenances with a convenient confidence, & shall at the encounter of any Lady or Ladyes whatsoever (especially if they bee young) & subject to our State of loue[)], bare themselfes erected & bee neither slow to speake or utter any becomming Complement out of a fear of a too suddaine retort, we being assured that ye wits of Ladyes or [are] not of that srenght [sic] & continuance which they are supposed to be, & if by chance any of our said servants bee not ready of Conceit, they shall not, as it hath been heretofore used, supply their discourse with oaths of any kind whatsoever, but it shall be lawfull for any, according to the most Received fashion in Court to catch at the loose haire of theire M^{rs} or play with their fanne, or shew her her owne looking glasse which shall hang somewher aboute her for that purpose, & shall thinke it noe disparagement or impaire to their wit to make a leap out of one discourse into another, especially if they find they cannot make their present good, for in such cases we will that custome prevaile & the present practise of the Court his [sic] to be observed by our said servants vnder paine of being thought Rusticke, & noe Fashionable or Courtly Gentlemen.

AN EDICT AGAINST RETAYLING OF COMPLEMENTS

Having found our Court of Love much backward in due Ceremonies and Court behavior and being inform'd y^t many of our said Court to the end that they may gaine some practise in Complements have taken vpp (many of them at the great expence both of time and drinke) from sundry sorts of men who pretend to teach them, or sell y^m rather, and for their better inablement as they (though vainly) suppose have practised such like Complements so taught them with certaine lewd weomen vsing about our Court commonly called Laundresses, Wee do straitly prohibite any attendinge about our sa[i]de Court to receive or Exercise such Phrase or Language in such manner with any such kind of People. Especially for y^t by the fore-saide Complements of many of our Servants wee have found that they have fallen into sundry inconveniences through their too familiar Conversacion with them And doe moreover charge all & every of our forsaide Servants to offer no kind of Courtly phrase or Complement to any inferior person or persons but to vtter them vppon fitt occasion. And then, only such as shall proceed from their owne shopp or brayne: Vnder paine to have their witts called in question Ore-tenus & to be examined by some of our Privy Counsell Ex Tempore whom wee shall appoint for y^t purpose.

AN EDICT AGAINST THE CONTUMACY OF MISTRESSES

Our welbeloved subjects having made sundry complaints to us of ye course, & lesse then mannerly entertainment of their mistresses, whom notwithstanding they haue endeavored as much as in them lay to demerit by faire service, & many applications, & having made relation vnto us of the great charge they haue been at of time, Jewells & severall sonnets, which they haue made in their honours, we in consideration of their sufferings have thought fit to inhibit any such Ladyes or Mistresses soe obdurate as aforesaid to use any conversation but only of perfum'd outsides, & such as shall sell their fames for a little vanity of talking; neverthelesse not prohibiting them to thinke that the kissing of their hands openly at a play or before Company to bee greater honour to them, then the true & cordiall service of a deserving lover.

An Edict against Poets Adventurers

Having taken into our Princely consideration the sundry abuses crept into our Court by reason of some adventurous persons that haue throwne themselfes into the Thesp[ian] waters without any mannerly consideration or forthought whether they were formed fit to touch it with the tip of their finger, wee being willing to meet with s[uch] an enormity doe hereby declare that noe person or persons whatsoever shall medd[le] in Poetry for that they haue gathered with industry phrases out of Shakespere Marston or the like or that they thinke they haue a pretty vaine of lov[e wri]ting, but only such as our privy Counsell shall find habile or fitt for soe high Calling; wee being informed out of ye great M^r of Poetry Horace, that the[re] can be granted noe such thing in nature as an indifferent Poet & though one may be a good Lawyer or Physition, though hee nether equall the king's Atturney or his Doctour; yet it fares not soe in poetry it being granted that n[o] mediocrity can serve a Poet; but that hee must be excellent in his kind; Besides the late examples of some who ignorantly venturing upon this Art, haue publickly demonstrated their want of grammatical skill, in joyning an Adjective Singular with a Substantive Plurall, & another publishing a long quantity upon the stage for a short, through his want of reading or advice before hand; & because by this reason the Common wealth is not as well served as it should be, for y^t he that is now against the will of all the Muses a Poet might haue made a pretty Gentleman Vsher, or an indifferent Courtier; we thinke it requisite that every man apply himselfe to what he is fit for, & leaue that which cannot become him, under paine of having all his Collections confiscated to the use of Chambermaids, waiting Gentlewomen & Barbers.

Bodleian MS. Tanner 88, ff. 121–122.

APPENDIX D

ACKNOWLEDGEMENTS

I AM indebted to the editors of the respective periodicals for permission to reprint the contributions following: *The Times*, 'An Elizabethan Madman and *Venus and Adonis*,' Apr. 21, 1939; 'A Holinshed Link,' July 8, 1935; 'John Shakespeare's Quarrel,' Oct. 1, 1931; 'Three Shakespeares,' Nov. 22, 1930; 'Burbage *v.* Shakespeare,' Dec. 29, 1926. The *Yale Review*, copyright Yale University Press, 'Ancient Pistol,' Autumn 1948. The *Atlantic Monthly*, 'Shakespeare and Mine Host of the Mermaid,' June 1933; 'Roaring Boys at the Mermaid,' July 1933; 'The Adventure of the Single Rapier,' July 1931. The *Sewanee Review*, 'Not of an Age,' Vol. 39, 1941. The *Spectator*, 'In Defence of Mercutio,' Aug. 9, 1947.